To Jerusalem

TO JERUSALEM

Devotional Studies in Mystical Religion

R. SOMERSET WARD

MOWBRAY

MOREHOUSE PUBLISHING

Mowbray
A Cassell imprint
Villiers House
41/47 Strand
London
WC2N 5JE

Morehouse Publishing
P.O. Box 1321
Harrisburg, PA 17105

First published 1931 by The S. Christopher Press
First published in this series 1994

British Library Cataloguing-in-Publication Data
A catalogue entry for this book is available from the British Library.

Library of Congress Cataloging-in-Publication Data
A catalog entry for this book is available from the Library of Congress.

ISBN 0-264-67356-5 (Mowbray)
0-8192-1627-5 (Morehouse)

Printed and bound in Great Britain by
Mackays of Chatham PLC

Series Foreword

THIS series is designed for the intelligent reader with a good grasp of reality and a generous amount of common sense who wants to know more about ultimate reality and the profoundest truths of human existence. Any religion worthy of the name is concerned with questions of meaning and value. Christianity is one of the great religions of the world and for nearly two thousand years has been subjected to the closest scrutiny by some of the finest intellects which have ever existed. The purpose of this series is to share some of the wisdom of the leading lights of the Church of England in the twentieth century who have written of the ceaseless human quest to make sense of the world and so attain the richest possible life — the Life which we all yearn to have in abundance but which too frequently eludes our uncertain grasp.

I first became interested in the great Anglican writers of modern times when I was researching my six novels about the Church of England in the twentieth century. The research involved not only studying Church history but familiarizing myself with the writings, theological and occasionally auto-biographical, of prominent modern churchmen. In the end I found a number of churchmen so fascinating and their writings so riveting that I quoted from their books regularly in my novels.

Unfortunately much theology dates, but I discovered there are two types of work which survive the passing decades: first-class explorations of the psyche (since the best writing on mysticism and sprituality is timeless) and first-class expositions

of classic Christian doctrine (since the truths being presented
are eternal). In the first four books in the Library of Anglican
Spirituality, Reginald Somerset Ward and Harry Williams
explore the psyche while Austin Farrer and Dorothy L. Sayers
expound doctrine, but inevitably there is overlapping as
apologetic shades into spirituality and spirituality illuminates
apologetic. All represent the Church of England in either a
traditional or a liberal form, and the next four books in the
series will continue to explore these two complementary facets
of modern Anglicanism.

It remains only for me to commend these authors, who have
given me so much enlightenment, and to thank Mowbray for
their decision to make these stimulating masterpieces available
to the modern reader.

Susan Howatch

INTRODUCTION
TO THIS EDITION

"ONE of the qualities of good spiritual writing is the strong sense of God's presence it conveys to the reader", states Norman Goodacre, who took over Reginald Somerset Ward's ministry of spiritual direction. "The writer provides material for meditation, intercession, quiet days and retreats: building blocks, in fact, for the construction of a spiritual life." The current widespread quest for the spiritual life by those both inside and outside the Church, a phenomenon which has been so notable in the past decade, has prompted a revival of interest in the Church of England's most influential spiritual director of the twentieth century, a priest whose writings exhibit both his mystical gifts and his down-to-earth understanding of the human soul.

Reginald Somerset Ward was born in 1881 into a clerical family, but a conventional Victorian upbringing was transformed when his widowed mother took him and her other children to live in Switzerland; Somerset Ward was then sixteen and had been withdrawn from his public school on the grounds of ill-health. Liberated from the constraints of such an education, he flourished, and it was in Switzerland that he first met his future wife, a young American woman whom he married at twenty-five after a four-year courtship. By that time he had taken a degree in history at Cambridge and had begun his career as a priest in London. In 1909 he became the Secretary of the Church of England Sunday School Institute, a job which in its peripatetic nature — he was required to travel all over England — foreshadowed his ministry as a spiritual director. He appeared to opt for a more settled existence in 1913 when he became rector of Chiddingfold in Surrey, but two years later he was responding to the call to a far less conventional way of life. Resigning his living with the approval of his bishop, he prepared to devote himself to spiritual direction. Since by this time he had not only a wife but two children to support, this was a brave move, but his faith was justified when a group of anonymous friends banded together to provide him with a house and income. Once his ministry was launched he used to visit fourteen city centres three times a year in order to see those who wished to consult him, and in between these demanding tours he would return home to Surrey to attend to his correspondence, to rest and to pray.

Prayer lay at the heart of his teaching. In his famous Rule of Life which he recommended to people in order that they might get the most out of their body, mind and spirit, he gave the first priority to prayer, the second to rest and recreation and the third to work. This recommendation proved unpopular with workaholics, but he was convinced that if the priorities became confused, the soul would fail to be aligned with God, with the result that unhappiness and impairment would follow. Somerset Ward, believing in a holistic approach to health, saw a balanced life as essential for progress along the spiritual way.

Today, when people are accustomed to the idea of counselling taking weeks and psychoanalysis taking years, it may seem surprising that Somerset Ward's interviews with those who sought his direction lasted about thirty minutes. There were two reasons for this brevity: the first was that most of the people he saw were not in crisis and merely wished for further guidance in their spiritual life; the second was that he was not a counsellor in the modern sense of a listener who seeks merely to be a helpful companion, but a counsellor in the older sense of a guide who shows a route to God to the traveller though never orders him to take it. In modern terminology the counselling was God-centred rather than client-centred.

It should not be assumed, however, that because he was not a modern counsellor Somerset Ward was uninterested in psychology. Many of his shrewd comments in *To Jerusalem* reveal his psychological insight. "So often", he writes on page 41, "when we are convinced that we have been real in some choice or action, we find in later years that our motives were far other then we claimed, and that we had not reached the bedrock of truth in ourselves." And in discussing the parable of the prodigal son he remarks: "For this young man was forgiven by the father against whom he had sinned, but the question still remained as to whether he could forgive himself." The importance of self-forgiveness in the healing process was an insight which is fully acknowledged today, but perhaps Somerset Ward's most innovative and influential belief was that fear was a major hindrance to the development of a healthy personality.

His six classifications of fear were: (1) Fear of blame or criticism. (2) Fear of guilt. (3) Fears about physical health. (4) Fear of sex. (5) Fear of failure, and (6) fear of insecurity. He felt strongly that it was basically fear that bedevilled people's lives, distorted their relationship with God and led to sin — which he saw as the making of a wrong choice. His job as a doctor of souls was to diagnose the hindrances of sin and fear in each patient so that these obstacles to health could be recognized, understood and mastered. It is of interest that he himself had a personal experience of debilitating fear when he was obliged to battle for many years against claustrophobia. Only when he finally understood its cause was he able to conquer it.

His profound insight into the human psyche together with the breadth and depth of his spirituality means that he still has a powerful message for the reader of today. *To Jerusalem* was the third in a trilogy of mystical studies, published anonymously and derived from the "Instructions", papers which he issued regularly to the people whom he advised. Wider in range than its predecessors, the book's section on prayer is of particular interest, and its sensible attitudes not only embody immense wisdom but bear out the belief that a gifted Christian mystic can be recognized by his — or her — sound grasp of reality. In an age where Christianity is too often misunderstood as exalting suffering and thus appealing primarily to masochists, it is also refreshing to see Somerset Ward defining suffering in this context as effort; there is nothing masochistic or unnatural about making the biggest possible effort to conquer one's difficulties and achieve wholeness.

There are two main difficulties facing the reader of today who seeks to explore the wisdom of Somerset Ward, but neither is insuperable. The first problem lies in the style of his writing. Athough we live in an age where information is conveyed by pared prose, Somerset Ward, educated in Victorian times, was accustomed to a more luxuriant, more leisured literary tradition. But once the adjustment to his style has been made, the value of the content can be clearly seen.

The second difficulty for the modern reader is that Somerset Ward appears to be oblivious of all modern biblical scholarship; he writes as if every story in the Bible is literally true, but since he was trained as a historian he cannot have been unaware of the work on the New Testament which was done in the first half of this century. The point for the reader to bear in mind when reading *To Jerusalem* is that the author is concerned here not with historical truth but with spiritual truth. He is presenting the New Testament stories as a series of meditations which reflect man's response to God in Christ and the workings of the Holy Spirit; he is using the stories to illuminate the great truths of human existence which are as relevant to us today as they were when he was writing in the 1930s.

Somerset Ward died in 1962, shortly after being awarded a doctorate in divinity by Archbishop Ramsey for his services to the Church, but his teaching lives on among those who knew him and it deserves to be more widely known today. "The Rule of Life was not, in his teaching and practice, a peace of legalism — an end in itself, or an impersonal strait-jacket that might crush the spirit", wrote one of his people, Canon John Townroe, in 1992. "It was a personal offering to the personal Saviour, and for Somerset Ward it was the master-key of life. He said: 'My experience of life teaches me the same lesson that I received at first — that the Rule of Life is the master-key of life.'" For all those in search of wisdom, in search of meaning and value, in search of lasting fulfilment, this book is a signpost, guiding all travellers who journey towards God along the spiritual way.

Susan Howatch

CONTENTS

TO JERUSALEM

I

THE CALL TO THE WAY

S. Mark xiv. 31.

"But Peter spoke exceeding vehemently : 'If I must die with Thee, I will not deny Thee.' In like manner said they all."

AND so should we, if the same question were put to us at the present moment. For, remember, there were two classes of people in the world that Thursday night —the multitude and the disciples. The former knew little or nothing of Christ and made no protestations ; the latter knew much and said with exceeding vehemence, "If we must die with Thee, we will not deny Thee." And we before God claim to belong, or desire to belong, to that second class. We protest that we desire to follow, and be taught by, our Lord Jesus Christ. So in the light of the events of that night I would ask you to face the meaning and the cost of being a disciple of our Lord.

A modern school of thought, which has its head-quarters in America, is given up to the glorification of self-assertion. The forceful, aggressive, certain man is the ideal they would hold up before us. The words of the disciples on this occasion would meet with their highest approval. Yet it is but a shallow creed. It will not answer to that great test which God has set for the race, for the nation, and for the individual—the test of humility. For, remember, our Lord's words were no vain hyperbole, when He said that the meek should inherit the earth. He was laying down a great and a literal truth. Only the humble can ever be strong. Now, humility comes of knowledge. Knowledge of two persons—God and oneself. The only way in which we shall ever be strong enough to be disciples is by being humble ; the only way we can be truly humble is by knowing God and ourselves. To something of this knowledge I trust that God may bring us, that we may learn what the disciples had not learnt, and be prepared to pay the price they would not pay.

I. Now, what was it that these men had not learnt? They had not learnt the meaning of discipleship. If only we can catch a glimpse of what it really means, we shall have gone half-way to avoiding their failure. True discipleship, then, is the last adventure left to mortals. Have you any spice of daring in you? Is there anything in you that rises to the call of a high romance, of a deed that shall flash out in a glorious blaze of lofty courage? If so, you can be a disciple : for it is not the explorers, not the captains of hosts, nor the knights of chivalry, who do the greatest deeds or take the road of the most glorious enterprise. It is the humble Christian who sets out to follow the road that leads over Calvary to God. Why is it, you may ask, that this is such a great adventure? It is because you cannot be a disciple without giving to God all that you have. Ibsen, in one of his plays, claims for God the motto, " Nought or all " ; but God's motto is far simpler, it is *ALL*. If you would gain all, you must give all : all that you possess, all that you desire, and all that you hope for. It matters not whether God lets you retain a part of your gift or not, the point is that *all* must be given. Let us have no more compromise ; we have had, God knows, too much of it in these days. We whittle down the call of Christ to suit the size of our houses, the amount of our incomes, or the interests of our lives. It is time God's priests rose up and proclaimed again the truth, that you cannot serve God in part and the world in part ; that the pearl of great price still goes to those who sell, not a part, but *all* that they have ; and that the disciple is not greater than his Master, but a copy of his Master. There is, there always has been, only one policy for the disciple, and that is the policy called " thorough." It is the general trouble with exhortations that while we agree with the principles set forth in them, we do not see the practical results coming from them. What would be some of the practical results of giving all to God ? It means giving all our time to God in the first place, and that means that our time must be consecrated by setting aside a considerable portion to prayer. Many Christians give two hours each day to prayer ; I do not think you can follow our Lord as a disciple with less than one. But the cry is raised, " My duties will not allow the time." They will if you make them, and if they did not, it should not be the highest but a lower duty that suffers. Or take our possessions. If they belong to God, it would not be too much to give a half or a quarter to His service. How many of us give a tenth ? Or take our talents and our reputations. If they are God's they must bear His hallmark. This means that all our so-called proper pride, our so-called rights, our position and rank, must be marked by humility after the example of our Lord Who was born in a manger. We must accept rebukes willingly, we must be pleased with criticism, we must in all things meekly give place to others. If these few scattered points help us to a truer idea of the great venture of discipleship, then God will have indeed blessed them.

II. It was not enough for the friends of our Lord to be, or to desire to be, His disciples. Their discipleship had to be tested. We all know the tragic story of how it failed. It is rather a suggestive thing that in the Gospel of Nicodemus, an apocryphal Gospel of the fourth century, the writer, giving an account of the trial of Christ, does not attempt to show the disciples, the men who had been with Christ, the men who had had the greatest opportunities, as standing up in His defence ; but relates instead how the simple, humble folk, whose sins had been forgiven and diseases healed, stood out before Pilate to speak on His behalf. He describes how a poor Jew stepped out from the crowd and said, " I was born blind ; I heard sounds, but saw not a face ; and as this Man passed by I cried out, ' Pity me, O Son of David,' and He put His hands upon my eyes and I received my sight." Likewise also said a certain widow, " I had an issue of blood and He stopped it." I think that the writer was probably true to spiritual experience when he made the humble, the suffering, and the poor the true disciples at the trial of Jesus ; for their faith had been tested. From the midst of sin and suffering they had acclaimed the Son of God, and having been once tested, their discipleship would be the better able to stand the greater trial.

So, if we would be true disciples, must we prepare
to be tested. And I know nothing that can help us
to pass this test better than to try to see why the
disciples failed. They failed chiefly because they had
not sufficient courage to follow their Master. They
could follow Him through ordinary hardships, through
a little contempt, a little giving up, but not through
mockery, scourging, and the Cross. And so, while
they fled, our Lord stood a lonely figure. There He
patiently stood, worn, sorrowful, alone, because no
disciple would follow Him. How many do you think
watched Him as He stood there alone? A few score?
You are wrong. A few thousands? You are wrong.
A few millions? You are still wrong. It was many,
many millions. All the souls who have ever heard
the Gospel, all the souls who will ever hear it. Among
that multitude we stand. We have the chance, as
they had, of stepping forth and taking our place by
His side if we have the courage they had not. Now,
why had they not the courage? In the first place,
because they had not counted the cost. They were
only prepared to give a little, not *all*. What are you
prepared to give? For, remember, we stand in the
same place as they did. We know no more than they
the nature of the test of discipleship; for it is a law
of the spiritual world that nothing certain can be foretold of this spiritual test, save that it will be quite
different from the one we expect. If we are to be
disciples we must count the cost of giving all that we
have to God. In the second place, they had not the
courage because they had not sought strength from
the only Source of Strength. It is an unconscious
irony on the part of the writer of the Gospel that in one

scene we find the disciples affirming loudly and without thought their constancy unto death; while in the scene which immediately follows, their Master is shown praying in an agony of humility for that same gift of constancy unto death.

How often have we prayed before the test? It seems to me this should be a daily prayer of every disciple: " Father, if Thou be willing, remove this cup from me; nevertheless, not my will, but Thine be done." Let us, then, face boldly the test which we must pass if we are to be disciples; let us face it with true courage which has been gained by counting the cost beforehand; by seeking in prayer that strength which our Father is so ready to pour upon us. And when that test comes we shall learn the great spiritual truth that there is really only one test for disciples, and that is the test of Calvary. Whatever be its form, in body, mind, or soul, all true disciples must follow the same road their Master trod. Stripped of all, in pain, in darkness, deserted and alone, they must hang upon the Cross as He hung there. Do I speak in pictures? If so, I speak only in pictures because there are no words literal enough to describe the truth.

This, then, is the call to discipleship sent to you.

And so it is that each time it is given, there sounds from before the Throne of God, where the great Archangels of the Lord stand to do His bidding, the blast of the trumpet which summons to the high adventure the band who will follow their Master to the end. Battered and worn, yet reckless and undaunted, they set their faces to the Hill of Calvary. A forlorn hope, a desperate band, weak, stumbling men and women, and over them and around them blazes the fire of the

Love of God, a light to lighten the world, as they leave all behind them for His dear sake.

The clock ticks off the minutes, each one equal to the last ; but in the clock of God there are some minutes which stretch out to eternity. Each of them is a choice. Dare you, will you, volunteer for the quest—the great quest, the last quest? Leaving all behind, will you take the road that leads to Calvary?

Count well the cost, and having counted it, take your place in the ranks, or leave them to pass on, for they cannot wait ; they have made tryst with a Captain Who brooks no delay.

See! the banner of God flies free, the ranks close up, and the army of the disciples of Jesus passes on to victory and the Cross.

II

MARKS OF THE WAY

(i) ADVENTURE

The Opportunities of Adventure

IT is inevitable that man's surroundings should exercise a continual force of suggestion on him. His environment tends to shape his thoughts, and, if his spirit is still free, the medium through which it is most often expressed is affected. It is permissible to think that an omniscient mind would see that every condition under which humanity lives has so many possible and varied results, that the balance for the life of the spirit is left unchanged. In other words, that we have the same spiritual chance as our forefathers, no more and no less. But if we leave this speculation, and concentrate our attention on some special aspect of the change which has taken place in man's environment, it will be evident that our surroundings have a certain bearing on our spiritual life to-day. Take, for instance, the habit which humanity has acquired of living in more or less square boxes, set beside more or less straight roads, with uniform pathways, and objects such as lamp-posts and pillar boxes at regular intervals. The result of this environment is the constant suggestion of limitation. We live, as it were, surrounded by loud speakers continually emphasizing the fact that we must go so far and no farther, that everything in life has its ordered place, and must fit into it. In short, we are asked to accept as truth, the idea that order is more important than life, that growth has to fit into a plan, and not a plan into growth. We are not (fortunately) here concerned with suggesting alterations in our environment, and if alterations were made, they probably would not change the ultimate chances of the spirit ; our object is rather to consider the effect on our spiritual life of this constant suggestion made to us. It is very easy, when everything we see round us is organized and limited, to fall into the habit of thinking that the same is true of the life of the Spirit. We are too ready to accept the suggestion, and to look on our spiritual life as one compartment of the whole, to be neatly arranged and ordered, with due care that it does not move outside its province.

It is interesting to note that our Lord, when He was called upon to describe the spiritual life, took, as an illustration, the one phenomenon in our daily environment which is least ordered and limited. " The wind bloweth where it listeth, and thou hearest the sound thereof, but canst not tell whence it cometh and whither it goeth : so is everyone that is born of the Spirit." Here was a revolt, with a vengeance, against the neat, pigeon-holed, precepts of the Pharisees and the idea of the spiritual life as a system. The wind, untamed, swirling in this direction and that, changing its force with every minute, liable to calms and to gusts, stirring everything on every side, was an uncomfortable symbol of religion in the soul for those who were precise and prudent. It was an illustration as awkward as it was necessary, for their day and for ours. Amidst the multitude of sermons and societies, of manuals and meetings, we have grown too tame ; we are losing the spirit of adventure in religion. Religion has been so classified by theology, history, and psychology, that there seems to be no possibility of new discovery. But, lo and behold, a little door opens in the soul, and we find ourselves in a country of which there are no maps, because it is a living country, made up itself of life and refusing to be bounded by lines and figures. Yet it is as hard for us as it was for Nicodemus to recognize the possibility of this discovery.

It is strange that the Northern nations, by nature so ready for physical adventure, should be so slow in spiritual adventure compared to the Southern nations. The Latin races seem only to be stirred to physical exploration by a spiritual stimulus. Christopher Columbus says in his will : " When I first undertook to start for the discovery of the Indies, I intended to beg the King and Queen to devote the whole of the money that might be drawn from these realms to the restoration of Jerusalem." At first sight it would seem that a religion which centred round the life of Jesus Christ could never cease to be a religion of discovery. The whole of His life and teaching is one mass of exploration and adventure, and in no point perhaps are our lives more unlike His than in this feature. Too often our real desire is to find a safe stopping-place where we can abide, rather than a base for further advance. Nevertheless, God has placed in us a certain restlessness, physical and spiritual, necessary alike to body and soul, which will not leave us content with stability. It is for us to stimulate and use this divine dissatisfaction. The moment we are aware of it, we are also aware of the feeling which balances it, the fear of effort or of failure.

We rightly distrust the strength of our wills, we are afraid of the reaction of depression if we do not succeed. Those who stay to argue miss their chance. Adventure requires an instant response, a certain recklessness, in those who are called, if it is to lead them to a new country.

But, leaving generalities, let us examine what this spiritual exploration really means in an ordinary life. To our normal mind, if we trouble to think about it, our daily life presents certain similarities to a prison. It is limited by certain conditions, necessities, and rules which seem to prevent any great or marked change. We have to get through a fixed amount of work at definite times, to be present at certain meals, and to get a regular amount of sleep. What opportunity is there in such an environment for adventure? Our mistake lies in thinking that the three dimensions in which we live are the only dimensions. There is a fourth, that of the Spirit, in which the opportunities of exploration are endless. We have to get up and come down to breakfast every day, but the state of mind and attitude towards life with which we do so is capable of infinite variation. The short time which is required for our bodies to go through this routine will suffice for a spiritual adventure to take place. We can make in those few minutes a conquest of self, and discover a miracle of grace. We have, perhaps, to interview someone for half an hour. If we approach the conversation with a settled conviction that it is part of the regular task to be got through as usual, we are losing a chance. Each conversation is a potential adventure, capable of momentous results. All through the day which seems so fixed and so ordinary, avenues are continually presented to us for a journey into a far country. At every cross road we pass there are miracles waiting round the corner. We can neither see nor use them unless we keep a living spirit of enterprise and expectation in our souls. Growth in virtues is a necessity if the likeness of our Lord is to become visible in us, but growth in virtues requires of us a constant readiness to try new ways of living. I cannot learn charity, that is to love my neighbour as God loves him, unless I make daily experiments. If I limit my efforts to what I have always done, my charity will be what it has always been. The Scribes and Pharisees laid it down that we ought to forgive those who offend us three times and no more. Our Lord showed us the way into a new country when He burst out with the response : " I say not unto thee, until seven times ; but until seventy times seven " : choosing the perfect number of seven as a symbol of the endless enterprise open to the adventure of charity. I cannot learn humility, that is, to see myself as God sees me, unless I am prepared to make and to take opportunities in each day for new points of view, new insight into my motives and my thoughts. Our Lord, when He set a little child in the midst of His disciples, was only pointing out to them a gate in their daily life which gave entry into a new and splendid territory, which it is open for all of us to explore each day. We are like sleep walkers, wandering with shut eyes, through a world full of opportunity for our souls. We admire S. Francis of Assisi, but we never recognize that all the astonishing things he did we can do on most days in our life, for the astonishing part of them was their spirit and not their expression.

And if we turn from the life of action to the life of

prayer, our need of the spirit of adventure is only more emphatic. How many people find prayer dull, who would consider a voyage to an unknown land thrilling? Yet the former is mysterious, unlimited, miraculous; while the latter is a commonplace. What is found dull in prayer is the little spot to which we are chained by fetters we have forged for ourselves. How readily we agree with ourselves that our prayers shall always follow the same round and be occupied with the same matters. The basis of a real life of prayer must be the conviction of its limitless possibilities. Intercession, Meditation, Worship, are all of them paths leading to the most varied scenes of the Spirit, if we have the faith to make an effort to follow them. We cannot expect too much from the love of God, for it is infinite.

Take these three paths and consider the way they open out. In Intercession we can discover that mysterious prayer of God, of which S. Paul speaks; can become aware of the wave of desire passing out from the Spirit of God through this world, and drawing human souls with an irresistible power. What limits can be named to this exploration? To enter into this prayer of God, and to make ourselves part of it, is to find new lights, and a new conception of the Nature of God. These discoveries we cannot perhaps put into words, they hang in a tantalizing way just beyond our powers of expression; but in spite of this we can learn them and make them part of ourselves.

If we turn to Meditation the same vista of enterprise is open to us. We put ourselves in a position in which the Voice of God speaking to us can be heard, now still and small, now loud and clear. What limits are there to the extent of the revelation which His love wishes to give us? Our meditations, like coral insects, are all the time building up cells, till at last we stand on the firm ground of certainty in the midst of the ocean of our ignorance. No navigator of old had the chance which is open to us in meditation of charting undiscovered isles. We are struck again and again in devotional books by sudden flashes of insight which we recognize by instinct to be true for all eternity. They are only the outlines of new lands discovered in the meditations of the Saints. There is no end to what God can reveal to us about Himself, no end to the freshness of the knowledge of Beauty, Truth, and Goodness in His Being, and it all awaits us in meditation, in an activity which is open to the humblest among us.

All that can be said of intercession and meditation pales before the possibilities of worship. Here the soul, leaving the anchorage of self, sails boldly, driven by the wind of the Spirit, into the realms of God. Each of the infinite qualities of God is an uncharted ocean. To desire the satisfaction of the Love, the Majesty, the Purity, the Generosity, the Humility of God (to name but the merest handful), is to discover a vast unknown territory. As we pray that these marks of God may be reflected back to Him from the life of this world, we find endless meanings and interpretations of which we had not dreamed. Or, if we take that great act of worship, the offering before the Trinity in Unity of the Living Memorial of the Passion in the Body and Blood of Christ ; the living representation and reflection of the Love of the Godhead held up before God, how infinite are the possibilities of insight. Day by day we strive to join in this supreme worship, gleaning, it may be, but the tiniest scrap of consciousness of what we are really doing. Yet each scrap is infinitely precious and fits into a whole which will one day form the Beatific Vision. Well may we desire of God the gift of spiritual ambition in our daily Communion, lest we pass such wonders by unnoticed.

In life and in prayer, alike, the opportunities for adventure which are put before us are stupendous. If we are to take them, or any of them, we must resolutely put away the suggestions of limitation which surround us. We must think of ourselves as spirit enshrined in a body, and not as bodies enclosing a spark of spirit. We must think of that home where the spirit only can find rest, and see the end of the journey while we yet travel on the road to it. Samuel Rutherford, who knew more of the travail of discouragement than most men, wrote finely : " Oh how sweet it is that the company of the firstborn should be divided into two great bodies of an army, some in their own country and some on the way to their country! If it were no more than once to see the face of the Prince of this good land, and to be feasted for eternity with His matchless glory and incomparable love, it were a well-spent journey to creep on hands and feet through seven deaths and seven hells, to enjoy Him up at the well head. Only let us not weary ; the miles to that land are fewer and shorter than when we first believed." It is very true that one of the reasons we are so slow to take the way of adventure is because we think so seldom of the hope of glory. There is no time like the present, and S. Paul was right to dwell on the importance of the word " To-day " when he talked of the journey of the soul. Why not, therefore, set forth this very day and try to find what is waiting all round you for your search? The pilgrim who sits on the heap of stones by the roadside, nursing his sore feet all day, shall never see the spires of Jerusalem, unless he listens to the call of adventure before night comes.

The Price of Adventure

S. Matthew xiii. 45.

" The kingdom of heaven is like unto a merchant man, seeking goodly pearls : who, when he had found one pearl of great price, went and sold all that he had, and bought it."

I can see that merchant man as the world saw him—prosperous, comfortable, business-like, and a man of method. He was, doubtless, what is known as a solid man of business, unmoved by whims and marked by a deep common sense. But, such is the mystery of human nature, he hid within himself a deep passion. He was a connoisseur of pearls. In some mysterious way, which he could not himself analyse, the sight of a pearl roused a desire which could not be satisfied till he possessed it. But the very depth of his passion made him particular, it must be no ordinary pearl ; such could pass through his hands daily and rouse no thrill save by their association with the ideal pearl of which he dreamed. And then one day chance rumour brought to his office news of a pearl worthy of his dreams, a pearl whose size, shape, and lustre proclaimed it *the* pearl, the one perfect pearl in all the world. I picture him sitting in his office, before his desk, weighing the pros and cons, arguing the matter out. " If I sell all that I have," he says, " my business, my home, my other jewels, I can raise just enough to purchase this pearl. Then what will happen ? Having obtained it, I can by no means give it up. It will mean that I shall be left without home or possessions. And after all, it is only a rumour ; the pearl may be gone ; I might lose it. What will the world and my friends say if I do it ? They will condemn my action as against all common sense, they will think I am mad."

Then in a moment there flashes through his imagination all that the pearl might be, and something rises from the depths of his being too insistent to be denied. " The pearl, the pearl only, I must have," he cries, " and whether I lose it or gain it I will pay the price for the one thing worth having."

Such, if I read aright, was the hero of Christ's story of the merchant and the pearl; and that hero was meant to stand, then as now, for the Christian. For the story is really the story of the inevitable bargain each soul must make. The bargain is truly inevitable, for the limitations of time and space force it on us. If we want to use created things in this world, we must in turn be used by them. Every use demands effort, and we must give before we can take; and since we are only in possession of limited time and energy, by reason of the limitations of our earthly bodies, we discover that we have to spend our capital to procure the benfits of created things. Now, since we have but a limited store of time and energy, it behoves us to use it for our best welfare; we have to choose on what we will spend it, we have to make a bargain with it; and if created and worldly things do not provide our best welfare, then we do but waste our little all in acquiring them. The question which decides what bargain each person will make is always the same. It is, " What do I believe is the real, the best? " Are the things my senses show me the true reality, the best in life? And if the soul says, " Yes," then the time and energy of life are spent on the acquisition of wealth or possessions. Or the man may turn to his mind and determine that his thoughts and imaginations are the true reality, the best. Then his time and energy are spent on the acquisition of knowledge or of power. Or he may belong to that class which turns unsatisfied from what his senses and his intellect have shown him, and demands a greater reality, a nobler best.

To this class the merchant man belonged. If the soul, making its inevitable bargain, turns away from earthly things and seeks an ideal, a pearl of unimaginable worth, then it is faced at once by the question of price.

What is the price that we must pay if we would have the pearl of great price as our very own possession, without doubt and without shadow of unreality? It is a very heavy price. It is the making of every interest or desire in life subordinate to one purpose. I mean this quite literally, and I mean it also when I say that very few of us are prepared to pay it. The fault with this generation, as with every generation before it, is that it is not prepared to pay the full price. It is prepared to put one or two other interests beneath religion, but not to make religion the greatest interest of life. And, let us look at the thing fairly, it is a hard price. The soul who has never said with Browning, " How hard, how very hard, it is to be a Christian," has not yet faced reality. Until a man has said with the servant in the parable of the talents, " Lord, I knew Thee that Thou art a hard man," I have not much hope for him. And it is not only a hard price, it is also a real price. I have sometimes spent time inventing endings for our Lord's parables, and the ending which I always choose for this story of the merchant and the pearl is this : " He died in a workhouse and was very happy." For I have never yet known a Christian who offered the price for the pearl of Heaven, who did not pay it to the full. It is

paid in lives which puzzle the world ; lives which seem
dull and monotonous, often full of trials or suffering, or
devoid of pleasures or excitement, and which are nevertheless, to all appearance, irradiated with a joy unearthly
in its depth and serenity.

We cannot consider this subject without hearing the
question, " Are you prepared to pay the price for the
pearl of Heaven ? " It is very easy, I am afraid, while
we are thinking of spiritual things, to answer " Yes."
But just think what it means. It means that religion,
the search for God as your own possession, is to be more
powerful than every other interest in life. It means
that it dominates all your cares about your body and
its needs, all your thoughts about the opinions which
others hold concerning you, all your plans for spending
time, and all your schemes for work or play, for business
or pleasure. It means being prepared to give up all the
things you are clinging to as the most important things
in your life, and putting in their place this one search
after God. I am not an idealist speaking in picturesque
phrases. I am telling you the sober truth about
Christianity, something which I know with an absolute
and final certainty, which no words can adequately
express, and which does not depend on myself.

Thus far we have studied the merchant and the price
he paid ; there remains—The Pearl.

We have in another part of the Bible the history of
a man who found the pearl. We call it the Conversion
of S. Paul, but it seems to me that conversion is a mis-
leading term, used often to describe a sudden change
instead of the gradual growth which is so much more
usual. At any rate, S. Paul's experience serves well to
show what is meant by finding the pearl ; for, mark

you, he did not only gain the conviction that there was a Son of God, or even that the Son of God was the Lord of his life, but he found himself *actually* and *really* in the unmistakable and absolutely personal presence of Jesus Christ, he *actually* and *really* talked to Him and heard His reply, knew what His Character and His Person were really like. This finding of God close to him, this intimate intercourse, this closest communion with Jesus, God and Man, which culminated in the third heaven, was the pearl which Paul found.

I imagine that to the merchant it was not the beauty and purity and lustre of the pearl which proved so strong a lure, for these it shared in their degree with other pearls ; but it was the fact that it was *the* pearl, the only one of its kind, the one perfect satisfaction of an ideal.

That is true also of this intimate finding of God. It is not one of many things, it is the only one, the only perfection of all that a soul has ever dreamt of Love and Beauty. There is nothing with which it may be compared, for there is no earthly thing which is like it, no human feeling which approximates to it. Those who have experienced it strive with stammering tongues to speak of it under many forms. As the converse of a father with a child, or of a lover with his beloved ; but it is significant that they turn from these similitudes very quickly, and unite in speaking of that love and of the return which it calls forth as fire or a flame—the which is obviously a symbol and not a similitude.

It is thought by the chance reader of these experiences that their writers are using picturesque and exaggerated phrases, but it is not so—their difficulty is that they can find no language literal enough to describe the reality. In such a " finding of God " is the only real and lasting satisfaction which this world holds, the only thing in which no end and no climax can be reached, the only passion in which accomplishment increases instead of killing desire, the only pursuit where infinite energy is combined with perfect peace. On earth everything satiates at last with the exception of love, and this finding of God is love in its superlative degree, in a degree not dreamt of in any other human experience, not to be attained by any other road save the one which the merchant followed.

And now perhaps, if God wills, we can see something of the great story which God's Son told in so few words. It would seem to mean that every soul is set like the delicate pointer of a balanced scale, wavering to this side or that, but at last judging and determining finally the real weight of the things which lie in the scales. On the one side are the apparently weighty things of earth—the gold, the power, the science, the comforts of body and mind, the life of home or workshop, the applause of men, and the opinions of society. On the other the pearl of great price, the finding of God, the reality of love. I feel a great pity for the wavering Christian, for it is an essential element of his choice that he cannot know the certainty about his choice till the pointer has declined this way or that and the balance is settled. The great archangels of God sit and wait while he decides which is the real, which is the best, for which he is willing to pay the price, the price of all that he has.

And if any should say that this is a desperate religion, a religion which might well frighten one by its struggle and fierceness, a religion very different from the placid and gentle religion which is so common and makes so

little difference—then I agree. I have tried a placid
religion, one which goes on the same from day to day
without visible signs of progress, without any appearance of reaching the goal at which it aims, which leaves
no deep scar or mark on daily life, and which does not
satisfy those moments of intense desire which shake the
soul—and I am tired of it. I reject it, because I cannot
believe that God would give to anybody an insatiable
desire for Himself if He did not mean to satisfy it. I
reject it, because if I cannot be brought by Him to the
possession of this pearl of great price, then there is
nothing else in the world which will satisfy me, and
therefore my life is wasted.

The pearl therefore I hold to be worth the price, and
this I know, that it is still in our midst, found by those
who seek it where they least expected it, given in
answer to the cry of desperation, here in our daily
life—

" For (when so sad thou canst not sadder)
        Cry ;—and upon thy so sore loss
    Shall shine the traffic of Jacob's ladder
        Pitched betwixt Heaven and Charing Cross.

Yea, in the night, my soul, my daughter,
        Cry,—clinging Heaven by the hems ;
    And lo, Christ walking on the water,
        Not of Genesareth, but Thames."

An Adventure

If I met Christ, while I was wandering in the lanes
and byways of the world, should I recognize Him?
Not by His dress, certainly, for He would be wearing
the most ordinary clothes, having always adopted the
dress of His day and of the men round Him. By His
face, then? The pictures of the Saints do not show that
you could recognize them as a class apart. We see
many faces every day which cause us to think they must
belong to good men and women, but we do not stay to
follow them. The crowds of Jerusalem saw no proof
they could recognize in the divine countenance of the
Man of Sorrows.

If I met Christ, while I was wandering in the lanes
and byways of the world, should I like Him? Absolute
truth is a very uncomfortable thing when we come in
contact with it. For the most part, in daily life, we get
along more easily by avoiding it : not by deceit, but
by running away from absolute truth. His conversation
would be absolute truth, and it would be difficult to feel
completely at ease in such an unaccustomed atmosphere.
There would be questions and statements which I should
like modified ; and, while I should enjoy the stories He
told, I should never be quite happy as to where they
were leading me. It is never pleasant to find oneself in
an insecure position, questioning all manner of things
which are generally taken for granted. We can never
go through life without clinging to a certain number of
prejudices, small, perhaps, but strong, and it would be
hard to find them being put on one side or overturned.
I might wish to turn the conversation from the line it

was taking, and it would be impossible to do so. It is not a condition usually of pleasant intercourse to feel ourselves palpably inferior to the person with whom we talk.

If I met Christ, while I was wandering in the lanes and byways of the world, would He notice me? I cannot but confess that there would be many things all round Him more worthy of His notice : a multitude of beauties in the created world, mechanisms more wonderful than mine, intellects and powers which would drawf mine. Out of the half million of pilgrims who flocked to Jerusalem for the Passover, to how many did He speak? While He was journeying, how many men passed Him on the road unheeding? And why should He, with a world to care for, delay His work to notice me? It seems by all the rules of ordinary thought that if I met Christ I should neither recognize Him, nor like to talk to Him, nor be noticed by Him.

Nevertheless, while we wandered in the lanes and byways of the world, we did meet Christ. We recognized Him at once because He was unlike anyone else we had ever met. It was no case of face or appearance, for there was nothing to be seen. It is true He walked beside us, suiting His pace to ours, and that at any time we could have stretched out our hand to touch His, but we did not recognize Him by reason of this. In the main we recognized Him by the fact He was nearer to us than anyone had ever been. With the best will in the world, and with all the love we had, there was always some barrier left with human beings. We could never enter into them, or they into us, so fully that there was no reserve left untouched ; but here was a penetration so complete that no obstacle was even left by which its completeness might be measured. There was nothing left to explain because it was all known, and not only known but shared. We only know people in the world in so far as we can enter into their lives and understand them, or in so far as they can enter into our lives and understand them. Here was Someone Who wholly and completely entered into us and understood us, and therefore we could not fail to recognize Him. We knew Him because He knew us.

There was another reason for our recognition. For when we had walked with anyone before, it had always been in this world; but in this walk we were aware that we walked in another world. This world was around us, and was visible to our eyes, but all its proportions had changed. The big things did not seem to matter, and the little things seemed important. Confidence and security had blotted out uncertainty and apprehension. No accidents could befall, nor was there any doubt as to what the future might bring forth, for all things were part of a perfect plan. Yet there was no unreality, for the world around us was real, but it had fallen into its place as a tiny part of reality and not the whole. We recognized Him because He carried heaven with Him.

And when it came to converse; we found at first it was all on our side, and then we noted that all our sentences were left unfinished. No sooner had the desire to say something bubbled up within us, than we found it useless to express it, because it was all known to Him. Being in the habit of earthly converse this was strange to us, yet in it we found an unwonted ease. We had forgotten that our fear of absolute truth was due to having something to conceal, and that when nothing could be concealed the fear departed. Our hesitation in conversation is due to what the person with whom we converse will think ; but when we converse with One Who knows us wholly, the fear is gone.

Nor was there any withholding concerning subjects we would have avoided. Apart from the fact that it was useless to avoid them when they were common knowledge, we found in ourselves a great enthusiasm to see them as He did. Not that we were under any delusion as to the tremendous difficulty in altering them, but we felt that we should face them strengthened by a partnership. If someone stands beside you and looks at your problems through your own eyes, sympathizing with your difficulties, and seeing them more clearly than you do, never shaming you by recalling past failures, it is hard to feel either frightened or discouraged. Yet in spite of all this sympathy and understanding we felt more strongly on the subject of these sins and failures than we had ever done ; not because they were wrong or had injured us, but because they could not accord with Him. There was a queer flavour of dislike to our misdoings, because they could not go out to welcome Him. But there was no lack of ease nor any paucity of stories in our conversation, for everything we looked at in this world became straightway a story. Whether it were what we call ugly or what we term beautiful, it no sooner caught our eye than it became a story full of meaning. Like one in the midst of a dream, we tried to fix them in our memory as they passed, saying to ourselves, "I will remember this," but they vanished with our Companion.

It seemed there was another reason for the ease of converse, for we became aware that we had never really lived in peace before. It was not the stillness of dead silence, for the noises of this world continued around us, but it was a quietude which made time of no moment. It was not that we desired to rest, but that we could not but rest. Rest and quietude were all around us, and penetrated us. We had no thought of when the walk would end, nor of what we had to do or say, for it seemed to us that we were in the midst of all Eternity, and that nothing could disturb it or make any difference to it. Plainly, therefore, in all such converse there could be no fuss or worry, nor any desire to question. How, therefore, could we fail to like being with Him, since all that caused fear, hesitation, or question in the conversation of this world was removed? It was strange, of course, to find that all we wanted to say was useless and unnecessary, but it was very restful.

But the greatest pleasure in this converse was the sharing. What is more delightful than to meet One Who fully enters into every feeling, thought, and plan before even it can be expressed? The sense of complete partnership doubles every happiness and halves every difficulty. And it would seem to be part of the fine courtesy of such converse that we are not allowed to feel our inequality. It is as if for the time He made Himself of our stature, so that we can no longer discern how minute we are. It was not hard to understand that He had become man and taken humanity upon Himself when in converse He could so completely identify Himself with the outlook of one life, one tiny existence. How could we have ever wondered if He would notice us? We knew, at our meeting, that not for one second in Eternity could He ever forget us. The word " love " is like the altar in the Church, half on earth and half in heaven. On earth it contains much that is emotional, exciting, vivid. In heaven it would seem that it is other than this. It is not an emotion but a state, having no variation and no climax, nor is it in need of expression. It is a state which unites and exists. It has no vividness, any more than the air we breathe, and is as changeless as the ether in which this world floats. It cannot change, it cannot die, it cannot move from that which it surrounds. It is as absurd to question whether it will notice that on which it is fixed as it would be to question whether there is any air around us. All the doubts we felt as we looked at ourselves vanished and ceased to be when we came into contact with this quality in Him.

In thinking it over we saw that we had given a strange importance to what we were, and but little importance to this quality in Him. As a magnet attracts a needle, so does any soul attract Him by reason of this heavenly Love. But it is one thing to be noticed, and quite another to be important. Yet here we found that all the little problems which would seem of no weight to other men were of interest to Him. By reason of His love He had so identified Himself with our lives that the question of the moment was His question also. Although He must have known that the problems were so petty as to be beneath all interest, He turned His gaze on them, and looked at them with us. It would be small wonder, in view of this, if we had been swelled with pride, and ready to look on ourselves as the centre of the world. But as He looked, we saw clearly the littleness of all our thoughts, not with any bitterness, but with a true recognition. They were so small that we were forced to turn from them. Whither, then, could we turn save to His interests, His life, His

desire ? The result, then, of any real experience of our
Lord is bound to end in worship.

We know really very little of the true nature of this
personal and conscious communion with our Lord. We
know it exists ; we can make some very good guesses at
some of the conditions which are requisite for it ; of its
mechanism, or how it fits into the complicated construction of a human being, we know next to nothing.
But of one thing we are sure : by reason of what has
happened to us, and of what is recorded again and again
by others, we are certain that such experience ends in
worship. From this fact springs an inevitable induc-
tion : since the consciousness of our Lord's real
presence ends in worship, and leads up to worship, it
must be that worship is its natural environment. To
those who seek this form of reality, and it is hard to
conceive of any who do not desire it, there is one place
where, more than any other, they can hope to find it.
That place is in the form of prayer which we term
worship. Owing to the paucity of human thought confronted by an Eternal Being, the term worship, like most
of the terms describing any feature of the spiritual life,
is vague and has several different meanings. In the
sense in which it is being used here, it means an attitude
and an activity. The attitude is that of unselfishness
towards God, the concentration of our interest and
desire and love on God rather than on ourselves. The
activity is the expression of this interest, desire, and
love by effort in prayer.

It is by changing the direction of our prayer, by
continual practice till a habit is formed, by perseverance
in spite of great difficulties, that worship becomes the
central fact of our life. And when that happens we no
longer say, " If I met Christ," but " When I meet Christ."

(ii) FAITH

The Struggle of Faith

ONE of the most marked contrasts between the Gospels and a modern literary work is the small place allotted in the former to the description of emotions and the brevity with which they are described. Regarded merely from the literary point of view, it is an intriguing method and one which modern authors might well copy, for it compels the reader to construct in his imagination more vivid pictures than the author could hope to paint. Yet, against this advantage, it is to be feared that our familiarity with the Gospels too often makes us lazy in the exercise of this co-operation with their authors, and that by our laziness we lose many a lesson which might assist us in the spiritual life.

There is one figure who stands perpetually in the background of the Incarnation to whom these observations especially apply. In all the pictures and stained glass windows there peers forth from the shadow or the background the face of S. Joseph, a perpetual interrogation to the spiritual experience of everyone who looks on it. What did this man know? How did he feel? What part did the events of Christmas Day have in his spiritual experience? We may well believe that there must always be doubt about any answers to the first two questions; but I do not think there is any doubt about the answer to the third. Pictures and windows unite in representing him as an aged man, and some of the early Dutch glass painters (if I remember rightly), through an incomprehensible antagonism to him, represent the saint as deformed; but they all, to my

mind, fail in the expression they give him. Surely one
thing we should be certain to find in his face would be
the deep lines left by an agony met and endured. In
the Gospel account, whatever else is left to our imagination, there stands out the supreme honesty of the man.
He is one who will do what is straight and clear to him
at any cost. And this is the man who is faced by one
of the most delicate and painful problems any man
could confront. To him it is not a problem he can
answer by any consideration of his personal feelings ;
he is bound by a Law which he holds to be a direct
revelation from God ; he has in his blood the strongest
and most persistent of racial traditions ; he is a descend-
ant and representative of the royal line, conscious of all
that such a descent entails in the rigid upholding of a
strict standard. Confronted by the situation he had to
meet, it must have seemed to him that there was no
escape. He must give the death wound to his own love
and to the woman he loved more than himself, or else
he must be a traitor to every instinct of his religion,
education, and birth. It was an alternative which could
leave no face unmarked ; which must have invaded the
inmost depths of his spiritual life.

The modern author would probably pour scorn on the
mode of thought which could not see the proper choice
in such an alternative, and would denounce as narrow-
ness the first intention of S. Joseph. Yet I think that
intention must have ranked before God with the intention
of Abraham when he bound his son upon the altar. We
might think that when he had reached the resolution to
put away his espoused privily, S. Joseph had sounded
the depths of his struggle. It was not so. There came
a divine message in a vision which offered him the

explanation of the tragic situation in which he was involved, and laid upon him the opposite course of action to that which he had chosen. The struggle had passed from this world—from the emotions and ties of human relationship—to the very citadel of the soul and had become the struggle of faith. For the explanation was not only one beyond the comprehension of his experience, but beyond the comprehension of any human experience. He was confronted with the dread question : " Can I believe what God has said to me ? " There was a new and more terrible alternative now before him. Either he must throw up his belief in God, and all that personal belief (which is our most precious possession) in God's actual contact with his soul, or else he must believe what all his humanity declared to be unbelievable. His spiritual and his human natures were at grips. If there were nothing else to make him a saint he could not have issued, as he did, from this warfare without attaining sainthood.

" Then Joseph, being raised from sleep, did as the angel of the Lord had bidden him." Behind the curtain of that short sentence there must have been fought a very armageddon, from which he came forth with the roots of his life torn up, with every conviction save one shaken, with his whole experience shattered in the dust, yet crowned victor. I doubt not but that his reward was immediate, for God does not delay in paying His debts. I see the man henceforth bathed in a childlike simplicity, ready to move at the slightest motion of God's hand, care free and joyous, released from the bondage of earth's fears, and knowing now and here the Peace of God.

If in the sanctuary of our soul there was a pictured

window wherein the history of our spiritual life was set forth under the symbol of the saints, who were protagonists in the struggles we have to face, I think S. Joseph would always figure among them, and in every soul. The divergencies of detail are so immense, the scenery of every spiritual battlefield is so different, that we may not at first be aware of the truth of this fact. Yet a little reflection on our past life will assure us that it is true. It seems as if God could not mould the human soul into the likeness of His Son without compelling it to go through the struggle of faith. It may come to some at the outset of their approach to God, and to others in the maturity of their religion, but none can escape it. In one life it may take place over an incredibly small detail, when in prayer we are taught that we must choose a line of action which seems opposed to all our tasks and desires and the reasons we have produced to support them. In another it may appear in some big choice which we recognize will be fateful for our future, where again we are called upon by the inner voice to reject the advice of friends and all the arguments we should consider as sound in the other matters of our daily life. Wherever it appears the question is the same : " Can I believe what God has said to me ? " Who, that can recall the tumult and warfare which ensues on such a question, will doubt that there were deep lines left on the face of S. Joseph ?

Why is it that God asks of frail human beings, who are tenderly nursing the feeble plant of their little faith, such a terrible question ? I think the answer is to be found in one of the most persistent of the dangers which threaten the soul. We all know it in some form or another. We are all conscious of layers of reality in our spiritual life. So often, when we are convinced that we have been real in some choice or action, we find in later years that our motives were far other than we claimed, and that we had not reached the bedrock of truth in ourselves. The struggle of faith is the means which God has devised for forcing us to get right down to reality, for compelling us to face the devious ways of our nature. In this struggle we are obliged to decide what we believe is the ultimate truth for us, and through it we learn a standard of reality which we can use as a test in other choices.

I cannot believe that God has less sympathy than man with the human being who has to answer the supreme question. Nay, I know that He has more. Yet it seems to be a part of the Divine self-limitation that the answer must depend finally on the deliberate choice of the human being. There may be many failures and many repetitions of the test, but in the end the man has to answer in his own voice and by his own will. He has all the help of the sympathy of God, all that patient waiting and constant reiteration can do, but no one can say the word for him. Our Lord seemed at great pains to impress on His disciples the need of watchfulness, and it would seem that this need is nowhere more imperative than in the case of these struggles of faith. They sometimes come upon us unaware, at seasons when we are inflated with the belief that we have made progress and are not as other men are. They always involve in some degree or other the effort of moving out of some rut in our life. They are always saluted at first sight with the cry, " It is impossible." And it is here that watchfulness is so great a help. If we keep constantly in mind that we have no abiding city on earth, we shall be the more ready to step forward from our resting place at the first call. The long drudgery which is so necessary a part of the spiritual life inclines us to settle down into rigidity ; it is watchfulness which keeps us elastic and ready to meet our test.

The part played by the struggle of faith in the formation of our final religious position is very great. Every spiritual life must look forward to a state of stability; a state in which, while there is development, it is, nevertheless, the development of what is recognized as a stable position. It is this consciousness of stability which comes as the first reward to the victor in the struggle. Something has been gained which can never be destroyed, which is eternal. Many people at first sight fall in love with the idea of a plastic foundation for their religion, but fuller experience always brings the craving for a fixed and unchanging basis on which to build.

A second reward emerges in a greatly increased strength of faith. By the very issue of the struggle we are convinced and our faith is confirmed, so that we are thereafter able to trust God in all manner of things which we could not formerly surrender to Him. There is no way of learning faith save by using faith. We cry to God to increase our faith, and His answer is to put before us the struggle of faith.

A third reward, and not the least, is a new peace. A great effort is always followed by peace, but in this peace there is something abiding. The smaller shocks of life are met henceforth with greater simplicity and less worry. When we consider how large a part worry takes in causing the sufferings of our existence, we might well esteem our struggle well repaid if this peace were its only result. One may well imagine S. Joseph as he looked back on his life, reflecting how easy his struggle would have been if he could have seen its results. Yet, judging from our own lives, such would not have been the case. We may know quite well all the rewards of faith, but the next struggle which lies before us will be as hard to fight as those which went before, for we must grow and we can only grow by being tested. So, as I look at S. Joseph standing in the background, I see in him a reminder of watchfulness, an inspiration of courage, and a hope of victory.

How God Strengthens Faith

Many minds have been exercised as to the relation between the animal world and spiritual life, and those who have given and received love in their relations with animals can hardly believe that so fine and noble a link betwixt man and beast has no place in God's scheme for the spiritual perfecting of His creation. The theory of evolution has taught us, with all due humility, to recognize the debt owed by our bodies to the beasts who preceded man on earth; and bids us remember the claims of ancestral blood and bone in our dealings with all living creatures.

Yet there is a higher authority to lead us to deal lovingly with the animal world. We cannot read the Gospels without recognizing the part played by animals in the life of our Lord, whether it be those which stood beside His cradle, or the ass which served for His triumph, the sparrows He had watched, or the sheep He chose to be the type of those He loved. With all nature and with all living creatures He was in sympathy. But it was given to one of these creatures to play a part in the Divine story which is deeply suggestive, leading us to speculations which concern our daily life and confirming the dimly understood lesson of many an experience.

S. Peter stood in the courtyard which divided the palaces of Annas and Caiaphas, and the hour of his testing had come upon him. It may be he had been congratulating himself on the cleverness and courage which had won him an entrance into the citadel of his enemies, for it is most often in moments of self-satisfaction that our testing comes. He had been warned in the most definite terms of what lay before him, and had been told the sign which would mark the crisis of his temptation.

Never was there a truer example of normal temptation. Though we may conveniently forget in our memory of past temptations the opportunities we had, yet at the time we are always conscious of a warning and of a moment of crisis when a choice is made. It is the habit of the human mind to seek relief from the pangs of remorse by thoughts of self-pity, and, above all, by the claim that we are the victims of injustice. Yet never I believe was there anything more scrupulously fair than our temptations, nor have we ever fallen into sin without deliberately overturning barriers which, left untouched, would have preserved us. The plots of many modern novels would seem to be based on the implicit assumption that temptation is both unjust and irresistible. This is not true to life. We make our own temptations ; but even when we have made them we are provided with means of safety, and always, though it be the lightning choice of a moment, we have to turn our back on these before we can sin.

The cock-crow in the courtyard of the high priest is a striking example of one of these means of safety, or barriers of defence, in the midst of temptation. For " as Peter was beneath in the palace, there cometh one of the maids of the high priest : and when she saw Peter warming himself, she looked upon him and said, ' And thou also wast with Jesus of Nazareth.' But he denied, saying, ' I know not, neither understand I what thou sayest.' And he went out into the porch ; and the cock crew." S. Mark, the secretary of S. Peter, must have got his account straight from its source, and it shows the sorely tried apostle in the midst of his temptation provided with a few moments of quiet and meditation. He goes apart from the crowd into the covered passage-way connecting the two palaces, perhaps to escape further observation. There, as he stands communing with himself, comes the signal, and the cock crows.

That sound, by the consummate skill of Christ's warning, recalls every word his Master said to strengthen him. If he listens he can save his honour through the centuries to come, he can prove his love for his Master. It is absolutely fair and just ; he sees in that instant where he is going, and what he is about to do. He will have deliberately to break down the barrier presented by his knowledge before he can complete his sin ; while, on the other hand, he has the opportunity to go down into the courtyard and avow his loyalty, and thus redeem all that he has lost.

It has been noted that this is a perfectly normal example of temptation, but the striking feature in it is the part played by the cock. No sooner had S. Peter withdrawn into the quiet of the porch, at the very crisis of his temptation, than the cock crowed. No sooner had he completed his sin than there came the second cock-crow. Take these two facts in conjunction with the words spoken by Christ during the walk to Gethsemane, and it is impossible for any reasonable person to think it is the result of coincidence, of chance, or accident. The cock which crowed is the instrument of God, used of set purpose by God. The bed-rock of most heresies, where it can be discovered, is found to be a denial that a loving God created the world for His glory. Yet as I think of the cock in the courtyard of the high priest, and of my own experience in many a temptation, I am assured that not only did a loving God create the universe, but also that He still retains His power over it and uses it, through much groaning and travail, for the carrying out of His plan for man and beast and every living creature.

Now it makes all the difference in any life if there is the conviction that God uses and works through every detail, permeates life, and is not outside it. Even though I heed not the crowing of the cock, yet if it is proof to me that God is close to me, it will make the effect of my sin other than it might have been. In the kaleidoscope, however you may twist the tube, the fragments of glass reflected show an ordered pattern. So is it in the life governed by the conviction of a loving Creator working through all the details of life, for in such a life there is no confusion of outlook, but only the certainty and security of a plan.

Again, our whole conception of the love of God is changed by such a belief based on experience. A love which watches from afar off can never be strong enough or personal enough to satisfy the craving of the individual soul. Love ever needs proximity, for it contains in itself the force of attraction. To know that the love and care of God enters into every object or condition in my environment is one of the strongest appeals which can be made to my love. It is one of the saddest facts in life that this certainty of the intervention of God's love in every tiny bit of life, being based on an individual experience, cannot be communicated to others. The certainty we have is built up out of thousands of little events, observed and explained in our own minds, linked by such clear connections that there is no room left for doubt, yet cogent only to us, and beyond our power to express in words.

There is, however, one factor which is essential before a man can attain this certainty of the intervention of God in all the details of his environment. " And the second time the cock crew. And Peter called to mind the words that Jesus said unto him. And when he thought thereon he wept." Behind the fall of S. Peter there was the background of years of devotion. This man had trained his spiritual being ; he had learnt to listen and to obey, and all those faculties which link man to the other world, the spiritual sphere, had been developed. S. Peter could see where another might be blind.

Here we catch a glimpse of the root of the confusion which afflicts all religion ; for if, without any preliminaries, every human being could discern the spiritual we could communicate to, and share with, all men the truths of God's dealings with man. It is however ordained, perchance because man values nothing for which he has not had to pay in effort, that spiritual sight and understanding shall depend on training for their development. If we are to see beyond the borders of the material world, to grasp its connection with the spiritual world, and gain some insight into the laws which govern that connection, it is essential that by prayer and a disciplined life we should educate the spiritual side of our being. S. Peter had done this and, however great his sin, it was not irremediable because he could understand something of its horror and could see what attitude he had to adopt towards it. For those who can hear the message of God through the cock-crow, sin is more terrible, but it is also less final than it is for those who are deaf. S. Elizabeth of Hungary wrote, " It is with us as with the reeds which grow by the river's side : when the waters overflow, the reed bows its head and bends down, and the flood passes over without breaking it. After which it uplifts its head, and stands erect in all its vigour, rejoicing in renewed life. So with us : we also must sometimes be bowed down to the earth and humbled, and then arise with renewed joy and trust."

Here, then, set forth in the history of S. Peter, we have a startlingly clear example of the intervention of God in our daily lives through the medium of His creation. This intervention would seem to be visible only to those who have tried by prayer and discipline to develop their spiritual being. For such it is alike a great proof of God's love and a great incitement to love God.

It may well be objected that there is a danger of our misunderstanding this use by God of His creation, that it might lead to superstition and a belief in omens. The answer to this objection is to be found in the fact that our Lord, during the walk to Gethsemane, had given S. Peter a warning. The cock-crow without our Lord's previous warning would have been only part of the ordinary mechanism of the material world ; in conjunction with His words it became an intervention of God in a human life. It is spiritual circumstances which reveal the difference between an ordinary event and a spiritual message. It is only (for the most part) in matters concerning which we have talked to our Lord that there is any revelation of His purpose through created objects. All through Holy Writ we find God using His intervention through His creation to confirm or explain, but only where His help has been sought, where the matter has been already brought to Him, where a repentant and surrendered soul seeks His help. Thus also Gregory the Great understood when he wrote: " The heavens knew their Lord, and forthwith sent forth a star, and a company of angels to sing His birth. The sea knew Him, and made itself a way to be trodden by His feet ; the earth knew Him, and trembled at His dying ; the sun knew Him, and hid the rays of its light ; the rocks and walls knew Him, for they were rent in twain at the time of His death. But though the senseless elements perceived Him to be their Lord, the hearts of the unbelieving Jews knew Him not as God."

In the lives of those who desire God, who strive to follow Him daily, there is ever a precious chronicle of the interventions of God, strengthening their love or increasing their repentance. It may be that we shall have to wait for the other life before we can know what great issues were determined by the help we received from this use by God of His creation ; but here and now we can see in it a means of increasing our love and trust, and a link for the stregthening of that personal relationship to our Lord which we count the most precious of all our possessions.

Faith and Sin

It is of the essence of a masterpiece of literature, that it does not finish up the subject with which it deals, but leaves open fruitful avenues for the further explorations of thought and imagination. How many are the journeys of which Dante's " Divine Comedy " has been the starting-point? The wider our study of literature, the greater must be our appreciation of the parables of Christ, for sheer brilliance of literary skill they have no equal, and the crown of their literary art is their simplicity. None of them fail to answer to the test of greatness laid down above. They all leave the hearer speculating on all manner of matters, because they are instinct with life in every detail, and each figure they introduce insists on going on living.

Among the figures of our Lord's creation, there is one who has a far more vivid life and personality than most of the human beings created by the same Lord to live in the world.

The Prodigal Son, the span of whose life is some twenty verses of the Bible, is known to us with much greater reality than any of the persons of whom we read in the newspapers. He walks in and out of our minds at intervals duirng our life, and occupies our thoughts, as one with whom we have a close intimacy. It needs no excuse, therefore, if we choose to meditate on that great climax of his life, the feast of his return.

We know what his father thought at that meal, for the interruption caused by his elder son called him away in the middle of the feast, and showed what manner of thoughts filled his mind. But I wonder very much what the Prodigal was thinking. Once the thoughts of a human being have reached a certain degree of intensity, it is no easy matter to switch them off into some other line. During his long and dreary journey home, the mind of the wanderer had been fixed on his own misdoings, and had hammered out the words with which he was going to greet his father, till they had become a refrain to which he marched : " Father, I have sinned against Heaven and before thee, and am no more worthy to be called thy son."

So through the din and uproar of the feast I imagine they still persisted : setting themselves to the tune of the music, and beating time to the clatter of tongues. For this young man was forgiven by the father against whom he had sinned, but the question still remained as to whether he could forgive himself.

There are many alien elements introduced into life by sin : for sin, while it twists growth, does not stop it. " My well-beloved hath a vineyard, and he looked that it should bring forth grapes, and behold it brought forth wild grapes." Sin does not prevent life from producing results, it only leads to the production of degenerate results. It is just these twisted results of a sinful life which make it so hard to fully accept forgiveness. So the Prodigal could not be blind to a ruined health, to a hostile public opinion led by his elder brother, and to wasted resources. Over against these was his father's forgiveness. His father had blotted out the past, but could he do the same ?

It would seem that this is a very common problem of the spiritual life, and it accounts for the fact that so many people, after they have confessed their sins before God, and received His message of reconciliation, are still without joy, and therefore without full gratitude. If to the mind of a Christian in such a case there come the words, " Perfect love casteth out fear," he will readily reply, " I believe that, but it is just because my love is proved so imperfect that my fear remains."

So into the Prodigal's mind in the midst of the feast might come the forbidden thought, " What shall I do if the longing for the open spaces, the jovial companions, the wild life, sweeps over me again ? " These two thoughts, the thought of the lasting results of sin and the distrust of our future actions, bred by past experience, form perhaps the most subtle temptation presented to the penitent sinner. Let us follow this temptation to its logical conclusion, which comes in the whisper of the tempter : " Since my life is entangled in the results of past sin, and my weakened will has no strength to guarantee resistance to future temptations, it is but hypocrisy to make a fresh start."

I think it was at the moment when the mind of the Prodigal had reached this point, that his father returned to the feast after the absence entailed by his interview with the elder brother. Doubtless, his face was clouded by the memory of his elder son's bitterness, while the Prodigal's face was darkened by his own thoughts ; yet as their eyes met the cloud and darkness lifted, and their love for one another overwhelmed all memories and all temptation.

This is the only real and final answer to the temptations which follow in the train of sin. It is because we do not look at God and His Love, but at our own lives, that so many of us go sadly away from our Absolution. " Perfect love casteth out fear," and there is only one perfect love, and that is the one just displayed to us.

If we will gaze on imperfect love when perfect love is revealed to us, we cannot be surprised if we have fear. I think that as the Prodigal gazed into his father's eyes at that moment, his thoughts changed, and his mind looked on a clearer vision of the future. He saw still the results of his sin, but he saw them surrounded by his father's love. Ill-health might bring much pain ; but he saw his body nursed, by constant care and his father's watchfulness, back to normal strength, and in the process he saw his love for his father increased. His brother's suspicion of him would continue, and be hard to bear ; but in bearing it he would have a new fortitude and a new humility, which would at last extort his brother's admiration. His money was gone, and for very manliness he would ask no more, and so he must stint himself ; yet the very hardship would be an incentive to steady work and ingenuity, and might well spur him on to heights he would never otherwise reach. " No," he decided within himself, " the results of my sin need not be final hindrances, as long as I have my father's love constantly with me to help me."

But still there was the haunting doubt of his own constancy. Again he catches his father's eye, again in it he apprehends that immeasurable depth of love. The feast and his companions vanish from before his sight, and he sees again the road by which he had set forth on his first reckless escapade. A long road, and a mile or two down it the well where he had stayed to rest beneath the trees. He looks into the future, and sees himself unable to bear any longer the enmity of his brother and his own impotence, again fleeing from his home, again wounding his father. Down the road he marches, driven by his pride and his longing to get away from everything, and again he turns the corner by the well, only to see his father waiting for him. He sees himself, helpless before that untired love, seated on an ass, and brought in triumph to his home, with yet one more bond of love uniting him to his father. And as the musicians burst into a strain of exultation his mind joins them, and he confesses that love is stronger than aught, and that in love is the final victory.

I do not think these meditations are in any way false to what God would have us think at Absolution, for the temptations arising from sin are age-long, and have not changed since the days of the Prodigal. Still, as I confess my sins before God, I see their results which apparently cannot be blotted out ; yet I must learn that love is an alchemist, and can transmute the base metal into gold, turning and twisting the results of my sin in the crucible of penitence till they shall become gold for my spiritual life. It is the spirit which moulds life, and there is no inevitable result which in penitence cannot be moulded into another shape. When I and the Prodigal think of something as inevitable, we leave out of account the fact that our Father's Love is stronger than anything on earth, stronger even than death. Every act has results, every sin has results, but those results are not immutable, for they can be transformed by love.

Nor is the truth any different concerning the weakness of our wills. It is there as a fact which we cannot deny, and no man, however sincere his penitence, dare be certain of a future in which he has to depend on so treacherous an ally. He knows within himself that his purpose is firm, but he knows also that he is so liable to change, that he seems to be a different man in the presence of temptation. Yet even this task is not beyond the power of love. There may be failures, but we can retrieve them. There may be falls, but love can arrest them. Each sinner knows that his chance of resisting sin depends on the maintenance of that simple discipline of life, different for each one, but vital for spiritual health. It is love which enables him to keep that discipline, or to return to it when it is lost. In the hour of temptation or in the moment of sin we cannot see these things, for our sight is darkened by our self-love; but at the time of Absolution God has made it clear, and we ought, therefore, to rejoice in the knowledge that love will triumph, and from our joy should spring gratitude.

In the spiritual life there is always a moment: that is to say, the lessons of experience in our spiritual lives always culminate in some definite crisis and some visible form; so that we, who see only by faith, may be assured of the certainty of what we have seen. In the long and arduous experience of repentance this instant is at Absolution.

Then it is that God makes clear to our limited human capacity His answer to our penitence in such a form that we have no excuse for doubt. It was when his father fell on his neck and kissed him that the Prodigal knew beyond doubt that he was forgiven, and whatever his doubts or temptations they were conquered by the love which was then revealed to him.

We notice that even after that revelation, his mind still followed the course it had pursued so long, and he did not at once realize that he was face to face with something greater than his sins. A certain Brother Rineiri fell a victim to a great and grievous temptation, nor could he rid himself of it, so that he abode in great despair, and at last deemed that he was abandoned by

God. While he was in such despair, as a last hope, he minded to go to S. Francis, thinking thus within himself : " If S. Francis will look kindly on me, and show himself mine own familiar friend, I believe that God will yet have pity on me ; but if not, it will be a sign that I am abandoned by God." So he set out and came to S. Francis, who at that time lay grievously sick at Assisi. And at that hour S. Francis called Brother Leo and Brother Masseo and said unto them : " Go ye at once to meet my son, most dear to me, Brother Rineiri, and embrace him on my behalf and salute him, and tell him that among all the brothers that are in the world I love him with special love." So they went and found Brother Rineiri, saying unto him whatsoever S. Francis had bidden them say. And albeit S. Francis was grievously sick, yet when he heard Brother Rineiri was coming, he got up and went to meet him, and embraced him very sweetly and said : " My son, most dear to me, Brother Rineiri, among all the brothers that are in the world, I love thee, I love thee with special love." And this said, he made the sign of the most holy Cross upon his brow and kissed him thereon, and said again, " My son most dear, God hath suffered this temptation to assail thee for thy great gain in merit, but if thou no more desire this gain, then let it be." Oh, marvel ! as soon as S. Francis had said these words, the temptation departed from the brother, and he remained altogether comforted.

And yet was it really a marvel, for S. Francis was only applying to his brother the method which God applies to each of us in Absolution ? Brother Rineiri and the Prodigal Son and we shall all of us conquer the temptation, which is the result of our sin, if we have more faith in the Love of God than in the sin we have brought to Him. The Liturgy gives us the only right order, for first comes Confession, then Absolution, and after Absolution the confortable words of God's Love and their call to faith. If we follow this order we shall know within ourselves that the brother who was dead is indeed alive again, and that he that was lost is found.

Faith and Fear

S. Matthew viii. 23–26.

" When He was entered into a ship, His disciples followed Him. And behold, there arose a great tempest in the sea, insomuch that the ship was covered with the waves : but He was asleep. And His disciples came to Him, and awoke Him, saying, ' Lord, save us : we perish.' And He saith unto them, ' Why are ye fearful, O ye of little faith ? ' Then He arose, and rebuked the winds and the sea ; and there was a great calm."

One of the most fascinating of the qualities of the sea is to be found in the impossibility of reproducing its atmosphere on land. Memory, pictures, photographs, all fail to give that reality which can only be recaptured on board a boat. So it is that these four verses can only be read to the best advantage while we are on a voyage.

It is all too easy, when we know the end of a story, to sum up the behaviour of the actors in it ; but it is only by putting ourselves in the place of those who took part in this scene that we can arrive at any true idea of its meaning. The pious echo, which is hidden in most of us, is only too ready to sum up this passage of Scripture with the comment : " Foolish men, they were quite safe in the boat." Such a verdict deprives the event of all its meaning. In spite of our presence on dry land, we must try to step into their shoes, and see the scene through their eyes, if we are either to understand it or to profit by it.

Why did these men behave in the way they did, crying out in panic, and giving way to despair ? Did they not know that the Christ Who was lying asleep in the boat was Lord of the world and all it contained ? There is no reason whatever to doubt their belief in their Master. Such belief is abundantly clear from the very manner of their appeal, for they cried : " Lord, save us, we perish." It is seldom recorded in the Gospels that Christ's disciples addressed Him as " Lord." This is one of the four or five occasions on which it happened before His resurrection. Nor do I think that if they had not believed in Him, and in His power, they would have appealed to Him at this moment ; they would rather have set to work on a desperate effort to save the boat. All the evidence points to the fact that they believed, just as we do, that their Master was Lord in heaven and on earth.

How, then, are the words " we perish " to be accounted for ? Standing in their place, in the midst of the storm, we can see that their faith had its limits. They could, and they did, believe up to a certain point ; but there they stopped. Faced by the forces of nature the limits of their belief became apparent. How could they reject the evidence of their senses ? There were the crests of the waves towering over the boat, threatening and impersonal. Here was the blast of the wind, sweeping down on the fragile bundle of wood which stood betwixt them and death. No faith, they thought, could be expected to withstand such realities.

It is curious, is it not, the absolute trust we repose in our senses ? Yet a moment's thought will show that they can be most untrustworthy. I look at a red lamp. I am prepared to swear through thick and thin that it is red and nothing but red. A fellow man, who is colour blind and shares his peculiarity with no small percentage of the race, will swear equally certainly that it is not red. If he puts absolute trust in his senses, he may become the instrument of a great disaster. So the disciples were prepared to trust Christ up to a certain point, but their trust was limited by the evidence of their senses.

And they went even further than this : not only did they limit the extent of their own faith, but they wanted to force the limitation on Christ. There is a certain touch of irritation in their cry, expressed as it is in the imperative mood. It implies that their Master has no right to sleep at such a moment. He must surely recognize that by so doing He is asking too much of them. He cannot reasonably expect them to carry trust to such a point. They are saying to Him in effect : " You must only require faith from us up to a certain point, and that point You must recognize as the limit, beyond which You cannot reasonably expect it." Such was the position the disciples took up, and it was just this position which brought down on them the stern rebuke of Christ. We can in some degree measure the seriousness of their fault in His estimation by noting that He rebuked His disciples before He rebuked the wind and the waves. He saw that their spiritual danger was greater than their physical danger. In the very order in which He dealt with their needs He gave them a lesson, for He placed the safety of their souls before the safety of their bodies.

If it be of little use to try to study this scene in the lives of the disciples without trying to put ourselves in their places, it is of equally little value to look at their lesson without finding in it our lesson. What is the meaning of this scene as applied to the normal experience of my life? At first sight it seems as if it had nothing to do with a normal experience. I am not often, nor usually, in a position of extreme physical danger. Yet a little reflection will assure us that the setting of the scene was no essential part of the lesson. The storm only served to bring to the surface a state of affairs which existed beneath, which had, in fact, become normal to the disciples. The lesson is concerned with the state and condition of the Apostles' faith ; a condition which was just the same in their ordinary daily life as it was shown to be in the storm. We are called upon to examine the state of our faith and to measure it beside the faith of these disciples in the boat.

It is common knowledge, to all who are interested in prayer, that the normal spiritual life is marked by ebb and flow. The life of prayer fluctuates betwixt sunshine and clouds, betwixt some degree of consciousness of Christ's presence and a feeling of dullness and inability. It is this latter state, this coldness and apparent absence of Christ in our prayers, which is the equivalent in our lives of the words : " He was asleep." Nor is it hard for us to find a similar equivalent for the waves and storm. It so often happens that these times of dullness and isolation in prayer are accompanied by testings or temptations in daily life. Many of us have poor memories for earthly things, but all of us have far worse memories for spiritual things. We forget what we thought we never could forget, those times when we were aware of Christ near us, and of the reality of God. So it is that, in these times of spiritual dullness, we are beset by many doubts. We begin to ask ourselves : " Is it real, or have I pledged my life to a dream ? " Close round us press the besetting temptations of our lives. They seem to us so strong that there is no chance of resisting them. We believe in the Son of God ; but in the face of such doubts, such strong temptations, such trials (so different, as we always say to ourselves, from those which others have to bear), we cannot cling to God any longer.

Then, having reached the limit of our faith, we proceed, like the disciples, to impose that limit on our Lord. " I have done all that is required," we say. " I have prayed, I have trusted, why am I still left without the conviction of God's presence ? " Few of us, perhaps, dare to formulate a complaint against God ; but many of us cry : " We perish." It is in this cry that the cause of our failure is to be found. Had the disciples cried : " Lord, save us," the storm would have been stilled and they would not have been rebuked. The rebuke was given for the two words they added to their prayer : " We perish." In those two words they asserted that their faith in the love and power of God was limited, and that God must be satisfied to accept the limits of their trust.

Having considered the limited faith of the disciples, and the same partial faith as we experience it in our own lives, it behoves us to find out Christ's judgment of such trust. Our Lord is very definite in His measurement of it. He addresses His disciples with these words : " O, ye of little faith." It is clear, therefore, that, in the divine sight, faith which is bounded by these considerations, and partial for these reasons, is " little faith." It is neither the normal nor the required amount of faith which God expects from us. The trust which cannot pass beyond the evidence of the senses, or the state of our feelings, does not satisfy His demand. A faith, or trust, which must for ever lean on the crutch of argument, will not suffice for the journey with Him. When the ebb of the soul is in progress, when doubt and desolation surround it, He requires from us a trust which will sweep aside the question, turn from the temptations, and accept the trials patiently. The half-way house of faith is to Him " little faith."

Any study of the periodicals and literature of our day makes it very clear that the delicate, wavering trust which the disciples displayed during the storm, is one of the marked characteristics of the present day. An anæmic faith which is unwilling to take any chances is very common among us ; and much which parades before us as audacity is only masked cowardice. It is of the essence of Christianity that we have got to take a chance ; that we must pledge our bodies, minds and souls in some degree to a distant probability if we are to be followers of Christ. It is in our nature that we should be perpetually trying to turn this probability into a certainty ; endeavouring to find mathematical proofs for it in prophetic books, or great pyramids, or spirit photographs. But the divine law is : that the nearer we come to reality in religion the less capable of proof it is ; the closer we approach to God the more faith we need to apprehend Him. It is unfortunate that nothing can replace trust ; no amount of services, or pious emotions, or austerities. Whatever we do will not save us from having to face the plunge into the unknown, from having to test the palpably insecure, if we are to come to God. Hard is it for a generation born in fear, and impregnated with anxiety, to face this demand of religion. It is little wonder if it takes refuge in expressions of doubt, and is ready to listen to any argument which will postpone the decision. It needs reckless courage in body, mind, and soul, to be a real Christian. Were it not so, the world would be full of them.

We must not forget that the rebuke to the disciples was not the last word our Lord spoke on that night. He spoke to the wind and the waves, and they were calm. That is the climax of faith. It comes off every time. When we are perfectly certain it cannot come to pass, when we are sure that there is no way out, faith confounds us by its results. In most cases they are not the results we foresaw or expected, but they are the accomplishment of what is needed to save us. There are few more potent answers to the terrors of death than our experiences with faith. There are few moments more uplifting in the spiritual life than those moments when faith justifies itself ; when the intervention of God is made visible to us, even though we can never make it visible to others.

Before every one of us, as we study the lives of the Apostles, there must loom up the momentous question as to the faith which is in us. Is it " faith " or " little faith " ? The choice as to which it shall be is in our own hands. No day passes without offering us the opportunity of trusting our Lord in some small matter, in prayer, or thought, or life. If we accept these daily opportunities, the hour which lies before us, the hour of crisis or the hour of death, will find us at peace, even though our Lord seems to sleep. And in that hour when we refuse to cry " We perish," we shall witness the triumph of faith, and the vindication of the love of God, which can only be known to those who trust wholly and not partially.

(iii) DISCIPLINE

The Purpose of Discipline

THERE is a strange and haunting sensation of which some of us are aware at intervals throughout our life. From early childhood to old age there come unexpected and unsought-for moments, when we suddenly feel there is something behind the visible scene on which we are looking, and that in another instant we shall discover it and know what it really is. The coming of this sensation in childhood has been admirably described by Hugh Walpole in " The Golden Scarecrow," but I think that, with the passing of years, it grows more vivid than it is in childhood. It is with some feeling akin to this mysterious sensation that I approach the subject of the power of God, manifested in the world. We know that this power is constantly at work around us ; we can see, as we look back, so many things that it has accomplished, and yet, at the moment of its working, we can never discover it, look as we will. We pray for God's help in some special piece of work we have to do, and in the doing of it we cannot discern what is happening ; yet as we review the matter in the light of later and fuller knowledge, it is evident that the power of God was working and changing things in a marvellous way. It may be that we are interviewing somebody, and we find ourselves in agreement with them quickly, and a solution of their difficulties appears quite easily. There seems to be no special and unusual sense of anything wonderful happening ; yet some long time after we may learn that that person came to the interview in a hostile spirit, with a mind firmly made up to oppose the right course of action, and that, to his surprise, the whole current of his mind was changed by some apparently chance word.

And the power of God is not only mysterious and invisible, but it is also tremendously strong. If we are oftentimes blind to the will of God, we are even more often blind to the strength of the forces which oppose it. We have, perhaps, gained by sad experience some knowledge of the self-love and selfishness in ourselves ; and, penetrating beneath the disguises of self-deception, have caught a glimpse of that stubborn, iron self-will which lies deep within us. It has sometimes seemed to me that when our Lord spoke of the faith which would remove a mountain, He must have been thinking of the mountain of self-will, for I have seen it as truly im-movable as any snowcapped Alp. Consider this self-will multiplied a thousandfold—a very Himalayan range— and you will have a small earthly picture of the forces which oppose the will of God in any matter of moment. Yet through all history, and in our own lives also, we see this opposition overborne and crushed by the vast power of God. I have often stood on the platform of some wayside station and watched a great express thundering through, shaking the ground on which I stood and dragging in its train a cloud of dust and debris ; and there has come into my mind the thought that if the power of God were set up against it, that express would come to a full stop instantly before my eyes. So vast is this mysterious and invisible force at work in the world that if it were plainly to be seen, man might be tempted to throw away the freewill with which he has been dowered by God.

Yet, at the very moment that we envisage this

majestic radiation of the omnipotence of God, we are confronted with a startling paradox, which we are tempted to call a jest of God, so grotesque does it seem ; for all this power of God, by His will, is used through the channel of puny human beings. It is as if Niagara Falls, instead of dashing its huge bulk of water on the rocks beneath, were only allowed to run through a thousand little taps. We can form many theories as to this self-limitation on the part of God ; we can see that if the virtues of earth are only tiny reflections of the character of God, there must be something infinite in His Nature from which our idea of humility is reflected ; but whatever the explanation, the fact remains that God uses His power through human instruments.

At first sight it seems as if it would be hardly possible to devise a more wasteful way of using the divine potency, yet a little reflection enables us to see that there are compensating factors in this method of use. It is evident, for instance, that since the power of God is sent forth for the benefit of human beings, by this method the benefit is doubled, for not only is the recipient helped, but also the instrument. If, for instance, there is a human being who has fallen into some habitual sin whereby his own life is being destroyed and the progress of the world hindered, and the power of God goes forth through some human instrument sent as a messenger to him ; then not only does that sinner benefit by the revelation of God, but the instrument also is brought to a new degree of reality in his faith and relation to God.

Again, we can see the benefit of this method of using human instruments, in the fact that it is the only method of which we can conceive, which would not destroy man's freewill. Unless the power of God were used through faulty human beings, its very immensity would kill all desire on the part of man to choose for himself, and that great decision, finally sealed when the legions of angels waited round the Cross on Calvary for the cry which never came, would be abrogated.

So the paradox, justified in these ways and in many others we are unable to see, holds good, and the vast power of God goes out into the world through human beings. But we are aware, both from our own experience and our observation of life, that there is a great difference in the capacity of these human instruments, and that this difference affects the extent of their use as channels of the divine power. I do not know of a more striking example in history of this fact than the story of S. Catherine of Siena. For seventy years the Popes had been living at Avignon, while Rome and Christendom alike suffered by their absence. It seemed as if no power on earth could move them from the luxury and wealth of their new home. The disasters which fell upon Italy, the petitions of the Roman citizens, the warnings of statesmen, the appeals of poets left them unmoved. The ever-growing danger of the gathering of the heresies which, like parasites, were sucking out the life of the Church, and the probability of their union under an heretical anti-Pope, which would have nearly destroyed European Christianity, had no force to overcome the Pope's selfish inertia. Yet, when all these arguments, set forth by priests and statesmen and poets, had failed, one simple peasant woman of Siena in three months accomplished the miracle, and the Pope returned to Rome. To any unbiassed mind it is evident that the irresistible power of God moved the Pope for the saving of Christendom. It is no less clear that it was because there was at last an instrument free from selfish motives, that that power could act with its full force.

It is a prime necessity therefore, if the power of God is to accomplish His purpose in the world, that there should be human instruments offering clear and unobstructed channels through which it can act. " Thy will be done on earth as it is in Heaven " is a prayer for ourselves as well as for God's glory. If, as is undoubtedly the case, we are called upon to act as instruments through which the power of God can act, it behoves us to be very clear as to the way we may remove obstructions and offer free channels for God's use. We know in a general way that it is love of ourselves which causes all the obstructions. We acknowledge this, but it will not help us much unless we can see in greater detail how it obstructs the power of God. If we turn to our own experience and think of our past failures, we may discern that the reason we failed was that we diverted the course of events from a growing and fruitful direction to a stunted or dead end. We deprived the project upon which we were engaged of its chance of living, and so it came to an end. The effect of introducing selfish motives into any scheme is to destroy its opportunities of growth, and so it gradually dwindles and dies. Suppose, for instance, you start some scheme for benefiting your neighbours ; it attracts others by its ideals, and the power of God working unseen collects round you all that is needed for its development into something far greater than you planned. With success there grow up in you the selfish desires of pride ; you want it to be entirely in your hands ; any criticism of the scheme arouses your hostility because you have identified it with your own reputation ; presently you squeeze out this person and then that, for fear they shall encroach on your central position. But this diversion of the scheme into selfish channels is fatal ; the work of elevating your reputation and satisfying your pride has no charm for others, nor has it any possibility of growth or development, and so the whole scheme dies down because you have blocked the channel through which the power of God flows. It is for this reason that the story of our lives is strewn with the debris of schemes which were failures.

Selfishness and selfwill in us block the channel of God's power, and deprive God of His glory and mankind of its help. Yet it is very hard indeed to make and keep the free channel for the power of God. It would sometimes seem as if our work offered more and better hiding places for self-deception than any other part of life. Our pride is covered by the plea that we are, after all, responsible ; our uncharity is hidden under the statement that we are defending the ideals of our scheme, our jealousy puts on the colour of zeal. Any Christian engaged in work for God and dependent on the power of God must be continually on the watch. Experience teaches us that there are certain signs which always give warning of the presence of self-love. The most prominent of them is hostility. The moment we begin to be angry with another person or organization we may be sure that self-love is blocking the channel through which the power of God flows.

Another sign is undue anxiety and worry. Where they appear it is certain that the work is no longer perfectly surrendered to God, but has become identified with some selfish desire or self-will of our own. The

answer to all such symptoms of deterioration must be
a fresh surrender. This means, in practice, a willing-
ness to have our work changed, to alter our plans, to
give up our position. It is a giving up to God of our
selfwill and a readiness to wait for what He will do.
And the answer to such surrender is always a fresh
outflow of the power of God. Through the channel
freed from obstruction the invincible force flows out to
do its work in the world, and miracles are wrought and
the glory of God is exalted. We can see dimly that,
in the final accomplishment of God's purpose, every
human activity will be translated into terms of worship,
and that therefore perfect work will become an adoration. One may dare to guess that it will be perfect
adoration, because when through unobstructed channels
the power of God flows freely, then God will be glorified
of Himself and those words of the Psalmist shall be
fulfilled : " *Exaltare, Domine, in virtute tua* "—" Be
Thou exalted, Lord, in Thine own strength : so will we
sing and praise Thy power."

Discipline and Power

The source of all the spiritual power which is to be found in the life of a Christian is in God the Holy Ghost. By the gift and will of the Holy Spirit, power is communicated to the soul, and therefrom penetrates to the whole life of the individual. It is therefore the first need of those who would be instruments of God on earth to develop their souls, to put the spiritual above the material, to seek the other world—the spiritual world—before the world of their senses, as they swing " wicket set " betwixt the two. But this spiritual power we so earnestly crave is subject to conditions which must be fulfilled before it becomes effective. Of these conditions, two are essential—prayer and discipline. Leaving prayer on one side, let us endeavour to see the relation between spiritual power and self-discipline.

It is very difficult to grasp the characteristics of a vague thing like power, and, above all, to express them in any simple form. Yet it is clear that in any kind of force, energy, power which we are able to conceive, one characteristic is evident—it is the tendency to push out, to spread, to dissipate. Take the lower forms of power —steam or electricity. The mark by which we know and use them is the same tendency to escape and to dissipate. The steam will only do its work when it is confined by metal and forced into a cylinder, and the more rigidly it is confined, the more effective it becomes. Electricity must be surrounded by non-conductors on every side or it will escape. Pass on to a higher force, a force not material, yet, as far as man can judge, unspiritual because it was wholly selfish. Consider the will of Napoleon. What power would it have produced without the harsh limitations and privations of his boyhood and manhood? Had he lived a century earlier, amid the surroundings of the court of the Grand Monarch, he would probably have grown into a prominent minister like Colbert. Amid the awful pressure of the Revolution and the savage necessities of his time, his power became effective because it was forced by harsh circumstances to flow in certain narrow lines.

The same law would seem to hold good of the Power of the Holy Ghost in us, and perhaps it is for this reason that there are so many good people and so few outstanding saints among us to-day. If spiritual power is to be effective, if it is not to dissipate into a vague goodness or waste itself in a wholly emotional religion, it needs the limitation, the confining strength of discipline. Such is the clear teaching of our Lord : " Strait is the gate, and narrow is the way, which leadeth unto life." S. Paul is acutely conscious of this truth and of its connection with power. " Every man that striveth for the mastery is temperate in all things," he says. This voluntary limitation, this setting up of rigid barriers in some parts of life, this forcing of the current of effort in some direction, is requisite in every life which is to be filled with effective power.

The consciousness of this necessity is innate in many persons, and they are apt to forget that it is only a condition of power and to think of it as the source of power. This was the conception which dominated early Hinduism, and has been frequent among the heresies of the East. Yet we must try to hold the balance true by acknowledging both the necessity and the dangers of discipline. The dangers attached to too much discipline are : revulsion, which must perforce come when power is too closely confined ; spiritual pride, when we mistake the condition for the source ; a degeneration of religion, which arises when what is artificial is given a higher place than what is natural, and rules usurp the place of love.

When we approach the question of the nature and method of self-discipline in any life, we are faced with a thorny problem. Many voices—crying " Lo, here! " and " Lo, there! "—claim that their own particular system of discipline is the only way of perfection. The Catholic Church, as its very title compels it to do, has laid down principles in place of systems. We shall do best if we approach the problem from another side and ask ourselves, " What is the spiritual and practical purpose of self-discipline ? " It is surely none other than to erect barriers against the constantly invading forces of selfishness and self-love.

From the particular point of view from which we are studying it, its purpose is to prevent the dissipation of power for selfish ends, where it becomes impure and wasted. Now selfishness is protean, and the best system of discipline to accomplish its end must be applied in a different form to suit the peculiarities of each person. Let us distrust systems which are founded on the fallacy that God made all men alike. Let us break down the habit of mind which argues that a system which helps your neighbour must, of necessity, help you. It is to meet the particular qualities of your own and my own personal selfishness, that the system of discipline which will really accomplish its work in us must be constructed. This is surely the meaning of our Lord's teaching when He said, " Take heed that ye do not your alms before men " ; " When thou prayest, enter into thy closet " ; "When thou fastest, anoint thy head and wash thy face." It was the privacy of spiritual discipline and its absolutely personal character on which He insisted. We should require, therefore, in the first place, of any system of discipline which we apply to our lives, that it should be personal, suited to our own individual needs, and restraining our own peculiar selfishness.

It is not uncommon with human beings to attempt to make a bargain with God ; to take some outside system of discipline and to say, " So long as I carry out this particular system of discipline, I shall hold that I am doing all that is required." The way to God, as Christ taught it and as we know it, admits of no such compromise ; it requires of a man more than acts ; it requires of him his whole being, his knowledge of himself, and his whole energy. The system of discipline required to make effective the power of the Holy Ghost is one which fits us like a glove and combats our own personal selfishness in the most effective way.

In the second place, the system of discipline must not only be personal, but also simple. Of all the treasure which Christ left to His Church on earth, the jewel which it has been most often in peril of losing has been simplicity. To have many rules means in the end to have none. The self-love of any human being is manifested strongly in only a few points, and it is to those few points that the discipline should be applied. Two or, at the most, three direct and simple rules, so constructed that they allow necessary exceptions, aimed directly at the root of selfishness, and capable of being carried out under any circumstances, will provide the best system of discipline.

Having thus seen something of the work and nature of discipline in its relation to power, it remains only to point out its spiritual importance. In this connection our attention is drawn to one of the most frequently repeated phrases in the Gospels. We find the phrase " that it might be fulfilled " about twenty times in the writings of the Evangelists, and in the majority of cases it refers to apparently insignificant acts or details : the choice of a particular village, the prohibition of a man to talk, the use of parables, the fetching of a colt, the instrument of execution, the gambling of soldiers for a garment, the sponge filled with vinegar, the spear-thrust after death. By the use of that phrase, these acts and details, which in themselves were so insignificant, became vitally important marks of the Divine will, making effective to the Jews and, after them, to the Church the power of Christ's life. There is here an analogy which helps us to comprehend the importance of those apparently small and insignificant rules which make up a system of discipline. There rises up in the mind of everyone who undertakes such rules a spirit of revolt ; at some time or other he has to face the attack of self which cries out against such rules as childish, making a fuss about details, small and limiting. Yet just as that phrase " that it might be fulfilled " before certain little acts, made effective the power of God to the Jews, so will the title of self-discipline given to these simple rules make effective the power of the Holy Ghost in the Christian life.

Again, I would have you note that those little acts and details we have mentioned appear most frequently and with the greatest force where we should expect them least. It is in the Crucifixion—the widest, broadest, biggest act in history—that they become most effective in power. So it is with the simple rules of discipline ; we keep them day by day, perhaps through long years, but it is at the great crises of our lives that they enable the power of God the Holy Ghost to become effective in us. How many a Christian who has passed comfortably through years of ordinary duty has failed at the crisis of his life through lack of power caused by the absence of discipline.

But for many of us there is an even greater testimony to the importance of discipline in our lives. The events of life can be viewed from two absolutely distinct points of view ; we can see them as occurrences happening by chance, dissociated from one another ; but in moments of spiritual sight we see them clearly and finally as links of one chain, steps in one definite plan. In such moments we are sometimes allowed to see the discipline of God being applied to our lives because we refused to apply our own discipline. In our glimpse of God's discipline we are most struck by its thoroughness. It is illuminated by mercy, but it is infinite mercy, and so it spares no effort to secure that each detail of the discipline be thoroughly and perfectly accomplished. In such moments we are made most truly aware that if we had carried out our own system of discipline, there would have been no need for this discipline of God, and that, nevertheless, this discipline of God sets forth the ideal of what our system of discipline should be. Such an experience forces us to ask ourselves the question, " If God is so intent that discipline should at all cost be carried out in my life ; if He is so careful that it should be thorough and worked out with scrupulous care, is it not a vital matter that I also should take up my

system of discipline and accomplish it perfectly?"
There is but one answer, and we should give it the more
readily because we recognize that it is not the discipline
itself which God wants, but the condition which will
render His power effective in us.

The Discipline of Mind and Will

I. *Cor.* ix. 26.

" I therefore so run, not as uncertainly : so fight I, not as one that beateth the air."

These words, though of course they refer primarily to bodily discipline, would serve very well as a description of what S. Paul understood to be the method of carrying out the choice he made at his conversion. On that occasion he discovered that there was a real person called Jesus, Who was divine ; he had to choose between his own way and his own self-will, or the following of this new Master. What did following the Master really mean ? The answer to this could only be worked out in life. As S. Paul worked it out, it became evident that in the words of this text we have a formula which describes his solution. I see S. Paul after his conversion faced by two very pressing problems, the first of which concerned his mind. He was in a most intolerable muddle, with all the pillars of his intellectual life falling in ruins about him. It was no mean edifice which, like Samson in his blind choice, he had brought crumbling about his ears, and it rested, like the house of Dagon, on two main pillars.

The first was the pillar of Rome. S. Paul was by birth a Roman citizen. This meant that his family were not just settlers in a Roman town, but that they had for generations been part of the town, respected leaders of the place. This was in no small town, but in Tarsus, the capital of a country, the seat of a university and of a school of philosophy which ranked third highest in the world. We cannot imagine to-day all that was meant by the words, " Roman citizen." They were a passport to safety and honour, a boast and a social distinction none could deny. Picture to yourself the mind of S. Paul in this struggle. He, an educated man, respected by his fellow citizens, a student of philosophy, pre-eminently a man with a career before him, settled in the Roman ideas of common sense and sheer logic, has now to accept the teaching of a wandering Preacher ; and in so doing to throw aside all common sense (for has he not accepted the belief that a man rose from the dead ?), and give up all worldly prospects. There are also indications that he had to face a terrible scene with his family. His nephew saved his life later on by revealing to him a secret which would never have been entrusted to a member of his family if they had not been known to be opposed to him ; and it is not by accident that so many instructions concerning the duties of parents and children were given by this Apostle, who was a bachelor. What a choice to put before a man. He was to give up the whole atmosphere of his mind, that very Roman essence with which it was soaked. No wonder he had to retire into the desert of Arabia to fight it out.

And there was the other pillar of his life, Jerusalem. He was a Hebrew of the Hebrews, no less a Jew for being so much a Roman, just as the true English Jew is no less a Jew because he is English. He had by his own confession an intense pride of race and religion, and an intense hatred of any disloyalty to the Law. To fulfil the Law, to carry out its least precept, he had left no stone unturned ; for God was known to the Jews only in the Law and served only by carrying out its details. I dare venture to assert that there was never a riot witnessed by S. Paul, during the course of a life which was singularly rich in riots, which made such a turmoil as this new surrender of his mind. He had to join those whom he had denounced as blasphemers against Moses and the Law ; he had to agree with outcasts and receive their teaching ; he had to point out the defects of the Church of the Jews to which he belonged.

It must soon have become evident to him that it was not enough to have a spiritual assurance, but that he must think out the whole matter and reach a clear intellectual position. And this he set out to do in a way which has benefited Christians ever since. He took what he was sure of, what God had revealed to him in his conversion, and worked it out in detail. He studied the teaching of Jesus, and enquired what it meant and how it would apply to each case ; and from his study there emerged a real belief. " I therefore so run, not as uncertainly." The runner in the Isthmian Games, to which he refers, had to run an oblong course round a central platform. A good deal depended on his choosing and following the right line. If he deviated from it, he would have to cover extra distance, and would be hindered by other runners getting in the way. S. Paul's method, once he had chosen Christianity, was to make sure of understanding what it meant in every direction.

It would seem to me that S. Paul's example has a special message to-day. As the standard of education goes up, more is demanded of Christians, and they can give more. It is required of every Christian to know what he thinks and understands about his religion. Vague generalities and pious phrases are not enough if we want to bear real witness for God. God alone knows the harm which has arisen from Christians who did not know what they meant by Christianity. Half the heresies and schisms of the world to-day are based on untested thought, which a little study and perseverance would have put right; and the other half on self-will, which would have given way before a little humility. S. Paul had no sympathy for a religion built up purely on emotions or on the carrying out of formal acts. Read the scolding he gave the Galatian Christians, who thought that their feelings and their ritual were a sufficient basis for their religion.

It is evident, then, that if we are to follow his teaching, we must, when we have made our choice to follow Christ, study the religion of Christ. We are members of His Church, and we have got to understand the teaching of that Church. Such study is not an extra in religion, it is part of it. But study in itself is not sufficient unless it is linked with prayer. S. Augustine has a fine sentence which sums up the Christian ideal of study. " Man," he says, " seeks by reading; he finds through meditation; he asks by prayer; he obtains through contemplation." And in another place he has a sound piece of advice to those who study religion for the purpose of controversy. " He will come to understand who knocks by prayer, not he who by quarrelling makes a noise at the Gate of Truth."

We should perhaps have to go back as far as the Reformation to discover a time when religion was so general an interest and so often discussed as it is to-day. Therefore the need is all the greater for Christians who, like S. Paul, do not follow Christ with uncertain minds, but by careful and prayerful study equip themselves as real and valuable members of the Church in which they have to bear witness.

I would ask you to note that in these words of S. Paul there is a great difference between the two pictures he calls up of the race and the boxing match. The advice he gives to the runner is to run straight and to know where he is going; while he advises the boxer to hit hard. In the next verse, speaking of his body, and continuing his illustration of the boxing match, he says: " I hit it hard under the eye," for that is the literal meaning which our version translates: " I keep under my body." The first half, then, of the verse refers to direction and the second half to force. And for this reason the second half brings us face to face with the second problem S. Paul had to confront after his conversion.

He had to deal with his intellectual questionings and then with the direction of his whole being towards that which he had discovered to be true. In this connection we are in the habit of speaking about " mind and will." Modern students of the mind are afraid that when we speak in this way we are splitting up our being into " faculties " which can act, so to speak, independently of each other. The will, we must think of, not as a separate faculty, but as the conscious self-direction of our whole being. For various reasons it was hard for S. Paul to tackle the question of thus turning his " will," the whole force of his being, to the service of the Lord Jesus. He had been educated in a world and a city where the Greek philosophy was dominant. The Greek teachers were always confused about the relation between the " thinking " and the " doing " part of man. They could never understand that a man may know and comprehend something without carrying it out in action. You will find the same difficulty in the minds of the

French to-day ; they seem to believe that if men or nations once know a thing they must of necessity act upon their knowledge. Yet you and I are only too well aware that such is not the case. S. Paul had to fight out this question, and to discover to his grief that a long training is necessary before his whole being turns in the direction which he knows to be right. How thoroughly he learnt this fact is best shown in his own words : " That which I do I know not : for not what I would, that do I practise ; but what I hate that I do." And even after he was clear that knowing the right and doing it were different things, he had still to fight his self-will and get control of it.

It was a hard fight, for this man had a strong personality. He knew what he wanted, and he wanted it very much. If Christ had not claimed him, he would have become one of the most bigoted and violent Jews of his day. His whole being blazed out at times, and if you would see the extent to which he won control over it, you have only to compare his dealings with Barnabas concerning Mark, and his dealings with Philemon concerning Onesimus. In the one case his will finds expression in a sharp contention, in the other in a tactful letter. I do not doubt that S. Paul found that changing his will to obey Christ was a much harder task than turning his mind to understand the teaching of Christ. The process must have begun very soon. He, a leader of men, blameless and unrebuked in the keeping of the Law, had to accept criticism from all sorts of people. He had to receive the contempt of the Romans, the revilings of the Jews, and, perhaps harder than all, the instruction of the Church. And so he learnt the real and only way in which the whole direction of our inner being is changed.

There is no sudden and easy way to change this deep force in us, it is only done by a multitude of small choices. You want to do the will of God, then you must do a multitude of tiny things day by day in obedience to that will. The Christian motto is : " Do the small things, and the big ones will take care of themselves." S. Paul won his way to the surrender of his will by constantly choosing in all sorts of small ways to give up what he wanted in order to do what he knew Christ wanted. Here is a matter with which we are faced every day. We have some little choice to make, it is of no great exterior importance, probably no one will notice what we do ; yet we know that we have got to choose between getting our own way, and giving it up in order to please Christ. It is on these little choices that the big ones depend ; and when we come face to face with some big temptation we shall be helpless unless we have trained our wills to go God's way in small things.

S. Benedict, who about the year 500 A.D. founded the first of the monastic orders, was one day taking a walk in a wild and desolate country when he came on a hermit, who, in order to force himself to holiness, had chained himself to a great rock. The Saint, far from admiring his methods, looked on him sternly and said: " If thou art truly the servant of God be not bound by a chain of iron, but by the chain of Christ." Now this chain of Christ, which alone will bind us and keep us from sin, is built of many links, and each of them is a small choice by which we turned our will to God's way. We cannot say that this turning of our will to God's service is easy. It sometimes seems as if it were harder to make ourselves do small things than big ones, that it would be almost easier to make up our minds to go to the stake as a martyr than to compel ourselves not to repeat that choice bit of gossip which will injure our neighbour in the eyes of others. Yet there is no other way by which a Christian can be trained.

The experience of S. Paul, the man who was so typical, and in many ways so modern, must be that of every real Christian ; for, once we are sure that there is a God and that Jesus Christ really lived and died for us, we have got to change both our way of thinking and our way of willing. We are bound to think out our religion and to study it ; we are bound to train our whole being to carry out what we have learnt concerning God's will.

S. Paul speaks of a prize which awaits those Christians who, having learnt the right direction, put all their force into following it. The word he uses for prize is " brabeion," which was a wreath of olive, parsley, and bay leaves, given to winners in the Isthmian Games. It is not without significance that from this word " brabeion " is derived our word " brave." The crown only goes to the brave, the Christian needs courage. In the life of S. Paul, in the need of the Church, in the call of Christ, we shall find a source of courage which will enable us to run not as uncertainly, to fight not at random ; that we may at last receive the prize which awaits those who with mind and will obey the Lord.

The Discipline of Friendship

Among the greater elements which influence human life, it is hard to find one more far-reaching or frequent in its occurrence than friendship. When we come to think of this great human factor, we are reminded once again of the great loss which we have suffered by the replacement of S. Paul's term " charity " by the word " love," which in our language has certain limitations of meaning that were absent from S. Paul's conception. These limitations have done much to obscure the root idea of friendship, they have led us to think of love and friendship as different things, whereas they are but differing manifestations of one and the same thing. In all true friendship everything which goes to make up love must be found. Friendship is love, and can only be differentiated from any other love by the fact that it has a different purpose. Each form of love is furnished with special characteristics suited for its special purpose.

In studying friendship and its place in the spiritual life, we are forced to seek the truth in the source of all truth. We are fortunate in having an unusually full account of our Lord's friendship for a human being, an account which shows also the contrast of that friendship with other human friendships. Each of us in life comes in contact with some fellow beings to whom we feel specially attracted, with whom we have some peculiar affinity of taste or nature. Our Lord in His perfect humanity recognized and consecrated this phenomenon. He chose a little family group of a brother and two sisters as His friends, and it is remarkable and interesting to find that they presented very sharp contrasts of character. Our experience will also bear this out, for the friends to whom we are drawn are often of very varying types. Our Lord would seem to have acknowledged the necessity of this, recognizing in it perhaps one example of that process of " filling up " which pervades S. Paul's epistles. It is certain that the binding together of very differing types of human beings by friendship does enrich each of them.

The friendship we are studying is revealed to us at a crisis. Lazarus, loved alike by Martha, Mary, our Lord and His disciples, was dangerously ill. We know but one fact about the character of Lazarus, the fact that he was lovable. Apart from the circle of friends we have seen, a large company of Jews showed their attachment for him, by attending the mourning for his death. It is also suggestive that each time he is mentioned it is to the accompaniment of hospitality, and we may conclude that he enjoyed the company of his fellow beings. The illness of this lovable man acted on his friends as light acts on a photographic plate, it made visible the nature and strength of their friendship. It is our common experience that there is no better test of the sincerity of love than sickness.

There lived in one of the villages of the north of England a miner and his wife. The history of their married life was not uncommon. They had lived contentedly enough together, going their own way and having their own interests, with little intercourse beyond the trivialities of the day. One night the wife, whose husband was on the night shift, was roused by the sound of men running through the village street. She heard voices shouting the news that there had been an explosion in the pit. As she waited in agony, leaning from her window, four men bearing a stretcher with a body covered with a sheet entered the gate of the garden. Persuaded that it was the corpse of her husband, all her pent up love burst forth as she cried aloud his name. The man was not dead ; but after his recovery he was wont to say that it had been worth while to suffer, because only at that moment had he realized how his wife loved him.

In like manner it happened that one day as our Lord was discoursing with His disciples, a breathless messenger announced to the group the message of the sisters, " Lord, behold, he whom Thou lovest is sick." It is at this point that the marks of true friendship are revealed. " Now Jesus loved Martha, and her sister, and Lazarus." S. John by these words seeks to emphasize the fact that it was no bond of acquaintanceship, but a deep feeling of true friendship which united our Lord to the household. Given this fact, and the circumstances of the case, we should have expected but one course of action on our Lord's part : that He would hasten immediately to Bethany to be with His friends in their trouble. It is, therefore, with something of a shock that we read the next words, " When He had heard that he was sick, He abode two days still in the same place where He was." Lazarus died about the time the message arrived. Our Lord did not wait for his death, but knew of it. It was no case of indecision nor of waiting for further definite news from a place which was only a day's journey away. The delay was a conscious and intentional act on our Lord's part, and it is for us to try to find the reason for it.

He knew the house of mourning awaited His comfort, He knew that it was possible to end that mourning,·

yet He deliberately abode for two days where He was. Again, we must emphasize the fact that He loved this family, there could be no doubt of His eagerness to comfort them, nor of His desire for their happiness. Considering the purity of His being, we are safe in saying that nobody ever loved an earthly friend more intensely than He loved that family. Yet He waited—the thing seems an absolute contradiction. The delay, and the fixing of the moment of return, were both caused by His love and His knowledge. He would only go at the moment when His visit would most help those whom He loved. His friendship was great enough to rise superior to what His friends would think, to what others would think. He was not satisfied to give anything save the absolute " best " to His friends. It was for this reason that He disciplined the natural impulse of His affection and waited.

There are few lessons in the true art of friendship more important than that taught by the action of Christ. The world is strewn with human wreckage through forgetfulness of it. How many are the lives with a secret root of bitterness or fear, which has its origin in undisciplined friendship. Too often the attraction of two human beings surges out in an emotional manner devoid of all control, dominated by the selfish desire to satisfy the craving of the moment. Such a friendship often does more injury to a life than a much greater sin.

The first lesson in the art of friendship is a lesson of discipline. A little thought shows both the reason and the rightness of this. Since friendship is love, its greatest mark must be unselfishness, the placing of someone else before oneself, and unselfishness is only possible by means of discipline, of warfare with selfish desires. The highest bond of friendship is forged in the fire of discipline, and it is true to experience to say that the greater the cost of the forging, the greater will be the friendship. A voluntary limitation of demonstration, a respect for our friends' individuality, a consideration of their highest good, are all marks of a great love.

We turn again to our Lord's example in search of another principle to govern and test our relationship with those fellow beings to whom we are specially drawn. After two days our Lord said to His disciples, " Let us go into Judæa again." To which they replied aghast, " Master, the Jews of late sought to stone Thee ; and goest Thou thither again ? " In Peræa was safety, in Bethany death. It is hard for us who know the sequel, to measure the cost of the decision ; but to those who were present it was quite clear that Christ was proposing to lay down His life for His friends. There was no limit to the manifestation of His disciplined love, all that was barren in it was cut out, that it might bear perfect fruit.

The mistakes in our human friendships are usually due to the fact that we give too generously what is useless to our friend, and are too niggardly in giving the more costly gifts, which are essential to his welfare. Too often we develop the weakness of our friends because we have not the courage to develop their strength. At the back of all appearances lies the truth that the measure of love is its costliness. To analyse one's feelings is the worst way of arriving at a measure of friendship ; to count its cost is the best way. Our Lord's measure of His love for the family at Bethany knew no limit, He was prepared to pay the greatest price a man can pay, He was ready to give up His life for it.

We sometimes complain of loneliness, of our failure to find any close companionship ; but, before we make such a complaint, we ought to ask ourselves what price we are prepared to pay for true love. The price of real friendship is often demanded of us in the very form we least expect or desire, the price of remonstrance or refusal, of sacrifice or surrender. There are solemn moments in all friendships when we have to face a decision on these points, and our decision determines the eternal nature of our love for our fellow being.

In the Gospel story we are now offered a contrast which further illuminates the subject. When the disciples had at last understood that Lazarus was dead they were overcome with despair. " Then," said Thomas, unto his fellow disciples, " Let us also go, that we may die with him." S. Thomas had missed the point of all our Lord's remarks about this event. Clinging stubbornly to the facts of the case and their earthly significance, Christ's words had passed over his head unnoticed. His friendship could only express itself therefore in despair, a noble despair, but barren and fruitless. He also was willing to sacrifice his life and pay a great cost, but in a useless way. A man in such a frame of mind would rather add to the grief of those he loved than alleviate it. He carried to their gloom only a blacker darkness, walking in the night he stumbled, because there was no light in him. How, therefore, could he help those he loved to stand beneath their grief ?

It would seem that we find in this contrast offered by S. Thomas the last essential mark of friendship. This man could not give the highest love because he was bound to the earth. He could not, for the moment, see beyond the material. He lacked the faith which alone could lift friendship to a level of spiritual reality. In our Lord's mind we can see that the spiritual welfare of the household at Bethany was the first consideration. The wait of two days was doubtless to enable them to understand more fully their loss, and to draw out more completely their faith. The tie which bound our Lord to them was knit most closely with their souls. If we would be true friends, giving ourselves to those we love, we must put the spiritual before the material in our relationship with them. Marriage or friendship, which is not based on some mutual spiritual outlook and ideal, can never reach perfection. If, as in the case of S. Thomas, our relationship cannot reach out beyond this world, it must at some point touch pessimism and despair, the forerunners of disaster. A high hope, an ideal, a desire for God, are the marks of the great friendship which illuminates a life.

As we look at the great lesson of friendship taught and enacted by our Lord, we must be struck by the fact that the character of this relationship lies so much in our own hands. The spirit in which we enter on a friendship, determines its growth. Too often we enter lightly and without thought into friendship, but if we consider it as a part of spiritual life, we shall be saved from this disaster. In such a case we shall approach it as a serious matter, striving to discipline it rightly from the start, prepared to give our best to it, however costly it may be, keeping it above the material in a spiritual sphere. If we can accomplish this by God's help our life will be enriched by the greatest gift to be found on earth, a friendship such as Christ gave to Lazarus and his sisters.

(iv) THE CROSS

The Suffering of the Cross

It is often helpful in considering a great problem to examine a special and concrete case of its working. From this concrete case the principles which govern the problem, and the right methods of working out its solution, may be discovered. In order, therefore, to consider the problem of suffering we will take one special case. It is the case of a man who, owing to the carelessness of his nurse, was dropped on the floor when he was a baby. This mishap caused an injury, which in later life manifested itself as a chronic and serious disease, which caused great pain. Under these circumstances the man asks two pertinent questions : " Why does God let me suffer ? In what way can Christianity help me in my suffering ? "

In answer to the first of these questions it is necessary to turn our attention to one of the most important factors in our human existence. It is one which we all forget, perhaps because we take it for granted. Even the lesson of the war did not really drive it home. This factor is our solidarity with the race of man. For most of us in daily life it is a habit, and supremely natural to us, to think of ourselves as individuals, isolated units ; or as moving only in the circle of family and acquaintances, and affected by very few other persons. Yet the real truth is, that we are all tightly bound up with the whole race, swerving with it in this or that direction, sharing in its gain and also in its loss.

We have too often forgotten the first and greatest doctrine which God came down to earth to teach—that

God was made man, not a man. We were taught in the Incarnation that provision must be made for the whole race, and not only for the individual. On Good Friday the Son of God taught the same lesson, that it was not only as individuals, but as a race, that we had to be suffered for on the Cross.

And at this point we can gain a fuller understanding by turning to our experience of life. We see quite clearly as we grow older, that every act of selfishness bears its inevitable harvest of suffering, by an immutable decree. This suffering, as we examine our own life and the lives of others, we see to be of two kinds, the one fruitful and the other wasteful ; and the difference between these two kinds is determined (as I hope to show) solely by the relationship of the suffering to the Cross. In this man's case the disease had arisen from the carelessness of a nurse, who dropped him when he was a baby, and thus produced conditions from which the disease arose. The careless nurse had doubtless done many selfish things in her life, had perhaps grown into a selfish habit of shirking work and effort, and the dropping of the child was probably the culmination of a long series of such acts. Selfishness brought suffering. We can point no finger of scorn at the nurse, for how many of our selfish acts are still bearing fruit in suffering we know not of. This we know, that each time in our life when we have acted selfishly, someone else has had to suffer somewhere, sometime, in some degree.

If we join this, our individual experience, to the truth concerning the solidarity of the race, it becomes almost intolerable to gaze at the result. The selfishness of millions of individuals is gathered into a black cloud of suffering overhanging the human race, and discharging on each member of it thunder drops of pain and woe. We cannot protest that this is unfair. We know well that it was no part of God's plan for the race. We have helped to create the cloud; and we knew, while we did it, that what we were doing was wrong. If we look at the position it seems hopeless, we seem to have raised a nemesis from which there is no escape.

The light only pierces the cloud when (as I love to think happened) one ray of the setting sun illuminates the Figure on the Cross. Here, and here only, is found a way of cutting through the vicious circle of human selfishness producing human suffering. For here was the discovery that, without breaking the fundamental law that sin means suffering, such suffering could be used to overcome its own cause.

Why has not the selfishness of the race before this brought about such suffering that mankind, unable to bear it, should commit race suicide? I believe it is only because the process by which human beings manufacture suffering has found a cure, and a way has been provided by which suffering has been used to redeem selfishness. God, by a lowliness of sacrifice which outshone all humility, used suffering to provide a cure and a redemption for selfishness once and for all on the Cross, and continuously by union with the Cross.

As I see it, the lowliness of God generated such a spiritual energy that anything which touched it, or came into contact with it, became filled with it (as a needle rubbed on a magnet) and began to act with it. Thus it is, that while all mankind shares in the suffering caused by selfishness, it is only Christians who have the secret of making their suffering redemptive and a cure for that which caused it.

The process by which our suffering becomes fruitful is twofold. First, there is the bearing of it after the manner of Christ in faith, hope, and charity ; and secondly, the joining of the suffering thus borne to the suffering of Christ, through faith and prayer.

Once this twofold process has taken place I believe that one of the most wonderful miracles in the world happens, for our suffering then is no longer passive. Suffering, where these two conditions are present, becomes active, an instrument full of energy, co-operating with Christ in His great work of restoring the race to which we belong to happiness and union with God, by the destruction of the virus of selfishness. It is not the wish of God that we should suffer, whether that suffering takes the form of sickness, disgrace, or any trial. We, as part of the human race, cause our own suffering, it is the result of the use of our human free will. God, since He is a God of righteousness and justice, must allow this suffering. But, since He is a God of Love, at the cost of an infinite sacrifice, He has provided a way by which that suffering may be turned into a triumph.

Thus it comes to pass that if this man will unite his suffering to the Cross of Christ by faith and imitation ; he will take part in the noblest vocation of them all, the vocation of helping Christ in His work of redeeming the race, of filling up the sufferings of Christ by union with Him and them. In the other world, if there are any commemorative monuments they will surely be erected to those who, by co-operating with Christ through His suffering, helped the world.

There is one point, however, concerning which we must make no mistake. Our sufferings in themselves have neither value nor merit. It is only in the fact that they are joined to Christ's Passion by faith and imitation that they can possess any value. The value lies in His sacrifice, and not in them. If they are not joined to His Passion they are worthless and wasteful. If they are united to His Passion, who shall be able to measure their value?

Such, then, is the answer I would give to the first of the questions. And, shrinking as I do from such suffering with all my being, I can yet find it in me to pray that such a man may reach the highest triumph open to humanity, and by his life may help mankind, and in his death may share in the victory and reward of Christ.

So far, we have looked only at the spiritual explanation of suffering. We have now to face the question as to how God expects us to deal with it. We cannot forget how short a space separates Easter morning from Good Friday. The Cross, if we may rightly say so of such a tremendous event, was only an event in a life, not the end of that life. It is noteworthy that, however else our Lord voluntarily limited His knowledge, He was always aware of the Resurrection, and repeatedly foretold it. If the Cross is represented in our lives by suffering, what is the meaning of the Resurrection in them? It can have only one meaning—a new life. In our Lord's case we find this new life was manifest in His body. All through the Crucifixion He had to trust in this as the result of His Passion, He had to look forward to it, however dark the prospect seemed. From His word to the penitent thief, it would seem that it held a prominent place in His mind.

I have tried to show that the secret of the right use of suffering lies in the Cross, and in a faithful imitation of Christ in His Passion. There seem to me to be two elements in the Crucifixion which are pre-eminent over all others : the elements of love and faith ; love for the human race, and faith in the love and power of the Father. I have pointed out how the first of these elements can be represented in our suffering ; and, since I am now speaking about the practical way of dealing with suffering, I would suggest that intercessions for other sufferers and for sinners should have an important place in a life of suffering, if suffering is to be united to Christ. But the second element is just as important. The faith in a new life and the triumph of God over selfishness and its results must be a constant feature in any suffering which is to imitate our Lord's. It will be seen that this means giving up entirely the doctrine that God means us to settle down to a life of suffering without alleviation. No suffering which does not look forward to a new life of freedom and strength can be after the pattern of Christ's Passion. If this man is to meet his disease rightly he must have an absolute faith that God means it to end in a triumph and the manifestation of a new life.

It is at this point that we are most aware of the limitation of our knowledge. We do not know the secret of life. In our Lord's case the new life meant a new life for the body ; and it would seem normal, since body and soul are united, to think that a new life must affect the body. We dare not, in our state of ignorance, lay down a positive affirmation concerning this ; for it is possible that the triumph of God over selfishness and its results can be manifested in ways and worlds beyond our knowledge. But we can affirm that suffering rightly borne ends in a new life ; and that it is the duty of any sufferer who is copying Christ, to look forward to this new life, to expect it, and to rely on it. However it may come, in whatever form it may show itself, I believe that it is the certain result of Christian suffering. I do not think it becomes us to lay down in what way this new life *must* show itself, but I think we *may* reasonably expect it to manifest itself in the body. All trust or faith involves of necessity the leaving of the nature of the result to God's choice, but it also involves the necessity of being convinced that there will be a result.

And here I would add that this faith is no sudden outburst, but the result of training and preparation. It may be that many sicknesses would be of much shorter duration if they were rightly used as training schools for faith. It would seem practical, therefore, for anyone, having this faith, to seek from God the manifestation of the new life. The ways provided in the Church for this are the Laying-on of Hands and Holy Unction. By these means of grace the gift of the new life is sought from God. They require faith, that is, the conviction that God means suffering borne in imitation of Christ to result in a triumph over selfishness and its results. They require also repentance, the removal by forgiveness of the sin which is so potent a cause of suffering. If these two conditions are fulfilled, I believe most firmly that through such means of grace the sufferer will receive a gift of life which will manifest itself in the way God sees best, but as a certain triumph over sin and its results.

The Triumph of the Cross

At the end of her ninth revelation the Blessed Julian of Norwich has placed this description of the glad giver. " A glad giver taketh but little heed to the thing that he giveth, but all his desire and all his intent is to please him and solace him to whom he giveth it. And if the receiver take the gift highly and thankfully, then the courteous giver setteth at nought all his cost and all his travail, for joy and delight that he hath pleased and solaced him that he loveth." In these words she sets forth an aspect of the Passion and Death of Christ which is too often neglected. It is inevitable perhaps, since we are human beings, that the foreground of the Crucifixion should be filled with the thought of our own sins. Yet it would be to the glory of God if they were the background and the love of Christ stood out the more vividly against them. It sounds like a contradiction of terms to speak of the joy of the Passion, yet the seeming contradiction is only a truth which has been obscured. We can the better understand this if we look at our own lives. When someone, of whom we are fond, is suffering we have no greater happiness than to alleviate his suffering. To many of us the thought has come, how great a pleasure it would be to us if by undergoing any pain we could save him suffering. Imagine this thought and feeling of ours magnified a million, million times. By so doing we shall get a glimpse of the joy which illuminated the Passion of our Lord. The emphasis laid by the Evangelists on the " loud voice " with which our Lord spoke His last words is no accident. It marks the triumphant joy of One Who has given His best to those whom He loves best.

Here on earth, anything associated with our bodies or environment must be very vivid. The pain, the shame, the toil of the Passion must have pressed themselves on our Lord most intensely. But to Him Who recognized the spiritual as the true reality, this joy of the spirit, in the accomplishment of winning a great freedom for those He loved most, must have been far more intense. Nor need we fear to follow this joy behind the Passion into even more mysterious regions. In all that Christ did in His Passion and Death the Blessed Trinity was involved. The love which our Lord was displaying was the love of the Father, and of the Son and of the Holy Ghost. Love is joy, whatever suffering it entails. The joy of Christ was the joy of the Blessed Trinity in this sacred hour. Hence it is that we can dimly see the reason and meaning of that wonderful offering which we make in the Holy Eucharist. We offer there to the eternal Trinity in Unity, the living memorial, the body and blood of Christ, which is the image of the love and joy of the Godhead. It is most pleasing to the Father to behold the only perfect likeness of His love. It is most glorious to the Son to see the living joy of His accomplishment. It is the satisfaction of the Holy Ghost to know the ever-working power of His gracious wisdom. It is the true worship of the Godhead to display the joy and triumph of God in its perfection. God can never be worshipped perfectly save by His own action, but when we are allowed to co-operate in presenting before God His own act we reach the greatest perfection of worship which we can know on earth. Thus it is the joy of the Passion and Death of Christ which alone explains for us the full meaning of the Eucharistic sacrifice.

The joy of God in the accomplishment of the Passion, as an act and revelation of Himself, is complete ; but, for its ultimate fulfilment, our co-operation is needed. As the Lady Julian pointed out, a great gift requires a great acceptance. The " pleasure and solace of him that He loveth " is necessary for the ultimate joy of the glad giver. From our own experience we know that there are few things in life which cause such suffering as the refusal, or failure to recognize, a gift which it has cost us much to make. Nor is it sufficient for us that the gift should be merely received and recognized ; if our giving is to bring its full joy our gift must make the recipient joyful. In spite of the fact that " the redemption of the world by our Lord Jesus Christ " finds such a prominent place in the General Thanksgiving, it is to be doubted whether the great mass of Christians either feel or express the joy they should for the Passion and Death of our Lord. In part this is no doubt due to the continuance of our sins which brings the cost of His sacrifice continually to our memory. In part it is due to the fact that we are not nearly conscious enough of the greatness or completeness of our absolution and forgiveness. In part it is due to the inability of our imagination to picture the final result of our sins from which we have been rescued. Yet none of these causes provide adequate reasons for failure to recognize this side of the Passion. They are all causes which place us in the foreground rather than the background of the Passion of Christ.

The Lady Julian with clearer sight saw in the very front of the Crucifixion the Triumph of God's love when she heard the voice of Jesus, our kind Lord, say to her, " If thou art pleased, I am pleased ; it is a joy, a bliss, an endless satisfying to Me that ever suffered I Passion for thee ; and if I might suffer more, I would suffer more." The true centre of the great scene of our redemption is what Christ felt and thought and not what we think and feel. It seems as if in our prayers and meditations about the Passion we should strive much more to penetrate this centre, and assuredly in so far as we do, we shall find there triumphant love.

Nor can it fail to aid us in this task if we make the attempt to see something of the nature of this triumph of the Passion. Human beings had set God an apparently insoluble problem. On the one hand, if they were to love in any full sense of the term they had to have freedom of choice. If they were to be capable of nobility, of merit, of reward, of being spiritual beings they must be free. On the other hand this freedom meant the possibility of wrong choice, a possibility of which they took advantage. Each wrong choice, each choice away from God entailed results, the automatic and inevitable results of actions separated from God. To all humanity this was taught by lesson after lesson. The Old Testament is an epitome of the lessons of one nation as representative of all. There is no season more fitting than Lent for the study of the Old Testament. In it we find the real causes of the Passion, the explanation alike of its necessity and its success. The summary of the process is given by our Lord in the parable of the husbandmen and the vineyard (S. Luke xx.).

Thus, then, into a world heedless of the ever-increasing results of its wrong choices there came the Christ, endowed with authority and power such as no prophet could have, to accomplish a task no prophet could do. The insoluble problem was to be solved by the introduction of a new life and power into the world, by the teaching at a great cost of a lesson which could not be forgotten, by the mysterious reversal of a spiritual balance which should alter the destiny of the world. It is because, like all eternal acts, this is a process in the midst of which we are involved that we are so often blind to its greatness and triumph. By its very nature, in that it was to provide a solution for the future, as for the present and the past, it was bound to be a process. No thoughtful onlooker in face of the history of the world can doubt that the spirit and the lesson of Christ has permeated, and is permeating, mankind. The solution of the problem is marching triumphantly on its way; but, to eternal eyes, which see a process as an act, and the end coincident with the beginning, the problem was solved in a moment on the Cross.

Yet to understand the nature of this triumph of the love of God in its abstract and general form is not sufficient to enable us to share in the joy of the Glad Giver. We must, as far as is possible, see the triumph actually in our own lives. In too many lives the memory of past failures is so vivid that the memory of the victories of God is dimmed. Yet who that reads these words can look back on life without being aware of growth, of increasing spiritual apprehension, of sinful habits growing weaker or being destroyed, of new conceptions of God and prayer. It is good to pray that God may win renown in us, it is also good to see that He has won renown in us. In seeing this we see here and now in actual fact the triumph of the Cross and Passion of Christ. We can rejoice with Him that, by the power of that wonderful sacrifice, transmitted to us in many ways, but especially through the Sacraments, His joy upon the Cross is justified, and that we are forced to share in it.

III

PROVISION FOR THE WAY

(i) PRAYER

The Origin of Prayer

THE great distinction which separates mediæval from modern science is to be found in the difference of their method. The man of the Middle Ages was always trying to explain objects by their relation to other objects ; whereas the modern man is always trying to explain them by their origin. To mediæval science the world was a jig-saw puzzle, to modern science it is a living growth.

It is for this reason that we look on human activity in a very different way from our ancestors, and this applies also to the highest of all human activities, which is prayer.

The scientific methods of our time have been applied to prayer chiefly through psychology and folk-lore. By analysis and archæological research an attempt has been made to trace back prayer to its source, and to explain it by the examination of its most rudimentary forms. We are too much the children of our age to doubt the efficacy of the method and therefore it becomes very important to seek an answer to the question : " What is the origin of prayer ? " Did it indeed begin by the necessity which men felt for propitiating the

destructive forces of nature ?   Was it in truth only the
sub-conscious reflection by man of himself on the world
outside him ?   Such theories may live for the moment
on the pages of a book, they cannot survive an instant
when confronted with prayer as we know it in actual
practice.

Prayer, as we know it, is different from any other
activity in life.   It has a vitality, an originality, a
growth which refute any instinctive origin.   It may
well be that those who have sought in these theories the
beginning of prayer have not gone far enough back.   I
would propose to you an origin of prayer as far before
the beginning of the human race as its fulfilment is
beyond it.   Research in our days, ever pushing back
the frontiers of the unknown, has tended more and
more to place the origin of life outside this world.   In
like manner those who pray, for prayer is a science in
which every Christian may do research work, are drawn
to the conclusion that their prayer has its source beyond
the limits of earthly existence.   There is, it seems, only
one origin for prayer which will satisfactorily account
for its characteristics and its peculiar qualities.   I see
the only possible origin of prayer in the eternal fact that
there are three Persons in one God.

When human beings discuss the nature of God there
is always the need to remember that they are using a
method (reason), and instruments (words), which are
finite, limited, and unequal to the task.   As S. Thomas
Aquinas says, " Reason cannot attain to God so as to
know what He is ; but it can know whether He is."
" But we could not know whether He exists unless we
somehow know, even though confusedly, what He is."
We can therefore only approximate to the truth ; yet

our approximation can be sufficiently true to establish principles which explain the way God works in the world.

We start from the fact that there are three eternal distinctions in the divine nature. These distinctions are not what we know as individuals, nor are they just characteristics, but something in the divine nature which has no equivalent on earth : something which is best represented to our human understanding by terms of relationship, Father, Son, and Holy Ghost. These three eternal distinctions in the divine nature, however much they may be mutually distinguished from each other, do yet exist in each other without confusion, and, as it were, flow into each other. It is to this special quality of the Persons in the Godhead that I would direct your attention. This inflowing, which is a perpetual condition of the Godhead, is due to the fact that God is Love. Ultimate and perfect Love so unites and flows through the Persons of the Trinity that they are one God. It was Chrysostom who first suggested what is probably the best earthly illustration of this inflowing of God. Inspired doubtless by the source of the river Jordan, he describes a spring rushing forth and forming a deep well from which the stream flows ; the same water, manifested in three distinct ways and perpetually flowing in and through each of them. So in God, eternal love is perpetually inflowing and outflowing, drawing and communicating, through the three Persons of the Blessed Trinity. It is this love which our Lord describes in these words, " For Thou lovedst Me before the foundation of the world," and thereby gives us a unique glimpse into the life of God, revealing an eternal love active in the depths of the divine Being.

This flowing stream of love in the Godhead is not,

and was not, cut off from man. From all eternity the purpose of the Incarnation, whereby God the Son became Man, must have included this world in the stream of the divine love. If through all eternity the Word had determined to take humanity upon Him, and to be clothed in flesh, it is evident that the divine love uniting the Persons of the Blessed Trinity included this world in its course. Such is the meaning of those great words of S. Paul, " the Spirit itself maketh intercession for us with groanings which cannot be uttered."

Perhaps you have happened to stand at sunset on some deserted stretch of sand, and have seen the tide coming in, driven onward by a relentless impulse, till it came to your very feet and seized some chance-flung piece of wood, and drew it away with an irresistible force into the vast space of the ocean, till its path was lost in the blinding glory of the sun. There you will have viewed in a picture that process which is forever going on : the infinite stream of the divine love eternally pulsing through the Persons of the Blessed Trinity, out from God, and drawing the world back into God.

It is in that tide of love that I see both the origin and the cause of prayer. It is because we are caught up by that love that we pray, and it is in the measure in which we surrender to that love that we pray well. When Christ revealed to His two disciples, as they walked to Emmaus, the part they had taken in an eternal plan they felt uplifted. Does not our heart also burn within us as we reflect that we, day by day, are sharing in, co-operating with, the very life of God, in prayer ? Specks of dust are we upon a speck of dust, yet so close to God that the living activity of the Blessed Trinity passes through us, and is shared in by us.

It is customary among those who seek to explain some
human activity by finding its origin, to deduce from that
origin methods by which the activity can best be
encouraged and developed. We cannot do better than
follow their example in this matter of prayer. It is
obvious at once, as we examine the source of prayer,
that we shall pray best when we are most closely identified with the great tide of the divine love. It is a
common reason for failure in prayer, that we are more
aware of the subject of our prayer than of its object ;
we are apt to think more of what we shall pray than
of how we shall pray.

The first and essential step in prayer is to unite ourselves with the stream of love and desire which is flowing
from, and to, God through this world. The preparation
for prayer is the most important, and often the most
neglected, step in our prayers. If you think about it,
you will realize that to unite yourself with the Essence
of all prayer, with the ceaseless tide of divine love, is
far more important than settling the details of your
petitions. And not only is it far more important but,
in reality, it settles the details. There is an amazing
difference, which can only be realized in practice, between starting out to make certain petitions to God, and
making those same petitions after we have endeavoured
to unite ourselves to the divine desire. We find that
such an endeavour changes the whole character of what
we ask. Much which we thought was important in the
petition or intercession drops like dross into the depths,
and we find ourselves seeking higher things than we had
thought possible.

The first practical result, therefore, of a study of the
origin of prayer is to make us examine very carefully

the way we begin our prayers. We should begin them
by an attempt to get away from the material world
around us, to attain quietude, and a state in which we
can be receptive to spiritual influences. I know no
method better suited to this purpose than some form
of meditation which directs our mind and desire towards
God. Let the meditation be as elastic and simple as
you like, on some article of the creed or verse of the
Bible. Follow this by a conscious effort to join yourself
to the love which is flowing from the Godhead all around
you. When you have joined yourself to that love, and
will to accomplish its desire, draw others into the same
stream, ask what seems to fit in with that divine desire,
or simply give yourself up to its working.

A second suggestion which arises from the consideration of the origin of prayer is concerned with energy in
prayer. We belong to an active race with a great sense
of responsibility, and, ever since the Reformation, we
have had drilled into us the necessity of doing our part
in religion, until it has often overshadowed God's part.
Thus it happens that for many earnest men and women
religion has become a strain ; their prayer has been
offered with a background of duty and a fear of in-
adequate effort, which has done much to destroy its
freedom and spontaneity. There is to be found a cor-
rective for this in the thought of the origin of prayer.
When we realize that the stream of divine love is forever carrying us and our desires into God, we are able,
by joining it, to relax the tension of our effort. I am
only too sadly aware of the dangers of sloth in prayer,
but I do not think those dangers will be real where a
conscious effort has been made to enter the current of
God's love. Moreover, I believe that not a little of the

difficulty found in prayer is due to the fact that our efforts so often diverge from the line of God's desire ; this divergence means a friction betwixt God's effort and our effort, which hinders prayer. It seems well, therefore, that we should learn to rely more on the energy of God's desire in prayer and less on our own feeble efforts ; directing our attention for the most part to identifying ourselves with the stream of divine love, and allowing our actual prayers to be carried along by that stream, rather than by our own activity.

There is an ancient legend, going back to the ninth century, which relates that during the persecution which followed the death of S. Stephen, the Jews seized Mary Magdalene, Martha, and Lazarus, and cast them into a little boat without oars, sail, or rudder, which was pushed forth into the sea. The unfortunate victims were carried out into the darkness of an approaching storm. For many days and nights they were carried by the waves, till one morning the rising sun showed them a fair land, and their boat came to rest on the sand not far from Marseilles, at a place still called " Les Saints Maries." There they landed, welcomed by the inhabitants, and converted the people of Southern France. Perhaps in that old legend we can see an illustration of what has happened to many an unknown soul. Bound and helpless in the midst of human infirmities, seemingly unable to pray, men and women have found themselves carried on the current of the divine love to a new land of light and power, wherein God has used them to carry out the purpose of His love. Of this I am sure, that the greatest works wrought by prayer have been accomplished, not by human effort but by human trust in God's effort. So I see the great circle of prayer interweaving, like those wheels of living fire which the Prophet Ezekiel beheld, passing through the glory of Father, Son, and Holy Ghost, out to this earth of ours, and back into the Godhead ; uniting us in our prayers with the very life of God, and making us in very truth sharers in the divine love and work.

Mental Prayer

S. John xvii. 1.

" These words spake Jesus, and lifted up His eyes to heaven and said, ' Father, the hour is come.' "

The stream of the divine love issuing from the Blessed Trinity passes also through man, and its current can most frequently be discerned in what is sometimes termed Mental Prayer.

If we have in the Lord's Prayer the standard of all Vocal Prayer, we have in this last great prayer of Christ the standard of all Mental Prayer.

When we read this prayer, putting aside all thought of the One Who used it, we cannot help but be struck by certain marks which stamp it. In the first place, it is so natural throughout—there are no forced phrases, there is no turning and twisting of words to make them suitable ; a sort of natural rhythm runs through it, and each sentence falls into its place inevitably. We note, too, that it is the simple expression of a series of thoughts and desires which flow like a river, serenely and in order, united together by the one tendency of the mind which produced them.

And again, we are almost surprised to find that though the prayer proceeds from one mouth, yet, it is in reality a conversation. Between each of its verses it would be possible to insert God's words. It is really a two-sided conversation, in which the words of one speaker are left to be understood.

And most of all, we are struck by the ascending scale of vitality that runs through it ; from the serene calm of its commencement, it seems to pass stage by stage to the glorious ecstacy of its conclusion, growing in vigour and power as it proceeds. To read this prayer is like seeing a coronation procession, which starts from the quietude of a palace courtyard, passes on into streets thronged with a cheering populace, and reaches its climax in some glorious abbey, where the crowned King is greeted by the thunderous acclamations of an innumerable multitude. I hope to shew you how these three marks of Christ's great prayer are to be found in their degree in all Mental Prayer.

In the first place, Mental Prayer is above all things the natural medium of communication with God. I am going to try to work out this point more thoroughly, for ignorance of it has deprived many lives of much comfort which they might have claimed as their due.

Why should it be so important that our prayers should be natural? The great principle which is our warrant for insisting upon it, is the Infinity of God's Love. We, with our poor, limited humanity cannot conceive of universal love. Our love is given in fragments, and shut up in many a prison cell, but the Love of God is boundless, and it embraces all. There is no corner in all this wide world where God's Love does not penetrate, no tiny hole or cranny which it does not fill. So often we fall into the mistake of thinking that God's Love is confined to great things. We forget that God is Infinite in His littleness as well as in His greatness.

In my own life I have known and realized God's Majesty most in the tiny things of life. It is when the sky opens and God's Hand is put forth to alter some trivial thing, to remove some tiny obstacle, that I have been most abased before the Majesty of His Love. Believe me, God's Love is so infinitely close to you, so incessantly caring for you, that if it were only visible to earthly eyes we should each of us stand this moment in the midst of a cloud of glory.

It follows from this infinity of God's Love that all the tiniest parts of our lives concern Him, and that in our communication with Him they all have their place : to leave them out is to narrow His Love. We can never meet His Love adequately in our prayers unless we are supremely natural, unless we talk to Him of all we are thinking, or feeling, at the moment.

We can only do this in Mental Prayer : that is by a conversation with God, where we do not try to put our thoughts into any set or grammatical form of words, but are content to think them towards God, in such disjointed phrases as may rise in our minds.

In all that I have known personally of our Lord, I have been struck by the fact of how much more natural He is than men commonly suppose. Those who write of Him, or attempt to picture Him, never make Him natural and simple as He really is. And in the same way I have always found that I have been nearest to Him when I have been most natural myself. You may have been struck at some time, in reading the lives or words of the Saints, by their audacity ; yet the Saints are not guilty of presumption nor of audacity, they are simple people, who have learnt to be natural with God.

If you would reap the full benefit of Mental Prayer, you must learn to make it express yourself to God. Speak to Him in it without strain ; think nothing too small or too foolish to bring before Him. Remember that His Love cares not for a part, but for the whole of your life.

In the second place, Mental Prayer is most emphatically two-sided. If this were not so the learning element, which is so rich a part of prayer, would be left out. It is one of the greatest defects of Vocal Prayer that there are not enough pauses in it. If we take earthly conversation as a picture of prayer, we can understand the importance of this point. We could never get to know people on earth if all our conversation were one-sided. It is surely only when they reply, when there is an interchange of thought, that we get to know them. The same holds good in Mental Prayer, for this way of praying is like a very close sort of conversation, where all the explanations and forms which make conversation so cumbrous are left out, because both parties understand them. Thus, those engaged in this way of prayer are never alone, for two persons take part in it, the soul and God.

Why should we think that God does not talk to us? The Bible is surely full of nothing else save the talking of God to souls. Prophets, priests, and just ordinary individuals like you and me are constantly talking and hearing Him, on every page of the Bible. If we are to judge by the Gospels, Christ talked far more to others than they to Him.

Now this is a matter of enormous importance to us, for it is vital that we should know God. If we do not get to know God, then what is the use of our lives, or what can they result in, save confusion and despair? Once in my life, when I was quite a small boy, I had an extraordinarily vivid dream, which remains always in my memory. I dreamed I was standing before a huge curtain, which seemed to reach up to heaven, and on the curtain were displayed all the things that ever happened or ever would happen. And, as I looked, it seemed to be utter confusion, a whirling madness. Then just as I awoke, I seemed for an instant to see that there was a key by which the whole curtain would fall into place and order. It took me many years to find out that the key was knowing God. I venture to describe the dream, because surely it is a picture of the soul looking out on the world and life. All seems to be confusion, and the only thing that can straighten it is to know God. Now we can know God best and most truly by listening to Him, and when we know Him all the facts of our life and of life in general fall into place and display the perfect plan of His Love.

It is for this reason that I would most strongly suggest that you should make pauses in your Mental Prayer ; that you should have short periods of silence when you try to listen instead of speaking to Him ; that you should allow the stream of divine love to carry you forward for a space.

And if you will persevere in this, you will find that He is indeed speaking. He does not speak in any words you can hear with your ears, nor even fully understand with your mind, but by sudden illuminations, by secret intuitions, and by convincing certainties He makes His meaning and His Will clear to the soul who is seeking the inner knowledge.

In the third place, it is a matter of experience that Mental Prayer is life-giving. The life of the soul is the most mysterious thing in the world ; that there is a life in the soul it is impossible to doubt, for the evidences of its existence are plainly visible. We see somebody suddenly change his habits, his way of thought and life ; and we cannot explain such a change except on the supposition that there is, deep within that one, some strong energy, full of vigour and fire, forcing its way out into action. In those moments, when spiritual sight

is clear, I seem to see the soul in the likeness of a tiny
spark, encased in the crushed clinkers of self, a glimmering light, a tiny sparkle. There is something pathetic
in its glimmering light. Then on a sudden it bursts into
white-hot flame, transforming the crust of self, and
giving forth the light which never shone on land or sea,
but which has shone through many a soul. So I picture
the life which enters the soul in moments of Mental
Prayer. For in such moments as God wills, a very flood
of vitality seems to be poured into the soul through this
way of prayer. And such life-giving as this is surely of
the very essence of communion, for by it God shares
His life with the poor and wretched soul.

We are blinded by our faithlessness to many of God's
miracles, and often we pass them unnoticed ; and not
the least of these miracles are the cases of new life given
in prayer. I have seen many people changed and made
new persons by the life which has flowed into them in
prayer. And I think you must have been conscious at
times in your life, when you have prayed very earnestly,
that you rose from your knees possessing a new and
mysterious vigour which was not there before, which
has come to you from bathing in the divine life.

Thus, then, in Mental Prayer we find the most natural
outlet for desire, the most close contact for learning,
and the truly vivifying channel of growth.

Each way of prayer has its dangers, and this way is
no exception to the rule. For in Mental Prayer the soul
meets the temptation (which arises from its very personal
character) of spiritual selfishness. Yet, after all, it is
very easy to avoid the danger, for a right use of intercession will keep the soul from spiritual self-love. A
further difficulty arises from the fact that so many souls,
having naturally so little power of concentration, are

apt to become vague in Mental Prayer. The soul does need by-laws for the regulation of its activity, and this difficulty cannot be lightly swept aside.

A third danger, more common than at first sight appears, lies in spiritual pride. The soul which has discovered Mental Prayer knows it has found something higher and better than Vocal Prayer, and begins too often to look down on those who are confined to the use of Vocal Prayer. For such souls is the lesson of the widow's mite. The golden piece which the rich man cast into the treasury was doubtless more beautiful than the " two mites," but it did not meet with as much commendation from our Lord, for He looked to the motive behind the act.

So also, He sees behind every prayer the desire which inspires it, and the Mental Prayer is weighed against the Vocal Prayer in the balance of desire. No soul who has experienced the two kinds of prayer can doubt which is better fitted for communication with God, but no soul who has learned the measure by which God judges our prayers will dare to say any particular Mental Prayer is of more value than the Vocal Prayer which is offered by another.

We grow, alas! so used to phrases and ideas that they lose the beauty which belongs to them ; but it seems to me that the very climax of beauty in this world is to be found in the reality of this way of Prayer. Think of it! Our poor, wretched, helpless souls, rapt out of themselves for a space, and entering, in trust and confidence, into communion with God ; the soul and its Creator, no longer separated, but together in converse, receiving and giving in intimate love, which needs few words, and is rather apprehended than understood.

And this is the way of Mental Prayer.

The Heights of Prayer

S. Luke xxiv. 51.

" And it came to pass, while He blessed them, He was parted from them, and carried up into heaven."

The stream of divine love issuing from the blessed Trinity passes through man and ascends again to God, in the path first trodden by the Master of all prayer.

I wonder whether, as the apostles watched the ascending Lord, the radiance shed by His risen glory seemed to make a golden path by which they could follow Him, whether this shining cloud of dazzling light into which He passed seemed to them the goal of some incredible journey which they were to take. The Lord had told them that He had taught the multitude in parables, and did He not teach His own chosen band in pictures? For it seems to me that we have in the Ascension of our Lord the picture of the final purpose of the great circle of prayer.

For what was really happening on the summit of Olivet that day? I think a chance spectator of the scene would, as sometimes happens, have got much nearer to the central truth than those who were immediately concerned. The central fact of the scene was that a human body had been lifted up from earth and carried into Heaven. God the Son when He came to earth became man, not only a man, but Man, that is to say He became a representative of the whole race of man ; a summing up, as it were, of every man and woman ever in the world. There was one great and all important difference between His coming down to earth and His ascending into Heaven, and that difference was

His human body. God came down from Heaven to earth, but God and Man ascended from earth to Heaven.

Further, it is just because He was Man, the summing up of all human beings, that when He returned to the Godhead, He carried with Him our humanity. Henceforth and for evermore it was impossible that man should be excluded from God, for man was in the Godhead, inseparably linked with God the Son.

The Ascension of Christ sets forth the goal and purpose of man. To be linked to God, drawn into and enveloped in the Godhead, was given as the final answer to the riddle of man's existence.

What then is the highest possibility of prayer? It is that the soul contemplating the Lord Jesus, and kneeling at His knees, should be lifted out of itself and united with the Incarnate Lord, and should enter into His eternal Godhead, which is one with the Father and the Holy Ghost.

It is not a theory about which I am speaking, nor a pictorial representation, but an experience, something which really can and does happen to certain human beings. Nor do I think there is any reason why any soul may not aspire to that which its Master proved to be possible by His final act.

We have seen the warrant for the highest possibility of prayer, but how can any soul attain to it? What manner of preparation is needed for such a goal? Hear the answer of one who knew by experience : " In weariness and painfulness, in watchings often, in hunger and thirst, in fastings often, in cold and nakedness." There is, alas! only one way by which the soul can ascend from the summit of Olivet, and it leads down a street

called the Via Dolorosa, and over a little hill called
Calvary, and through a garden wherein is a tomb. Yes,
it is true there is no other way to the heights of prayer
than the one the Master of prayer took Himself. There
were, no doubt, a thousand ways in which Christ could
have changed the world; the evil one suggested a few
of them at the Mount of Temptation, but the only one
He chose must be " the best." He chose deliberately
and finally the way of suffering, and He chose it not
for Himself only, but as the Representative of men.
Our human words are very limited and very often do
not express what we would say. I do not know if
I strain the word suffering beyond its right meaning,
but by it I mean *effort* carried to its utmost *degree*;
the effort which is terrible because it is so great, and
intensely painful because it is so long.

Now Christ taught us that the disciple is not greater
than his Master, but a copy of his Master. The disciple
who has vowed himself to follow his Lord in prayer
can take no other way than the way of suffering; you
cannot, therefore, come to this degree of prayer suddenly or by accident; it comes only after a long training
and many a bitter experience; the training is necessary
to teach you how to make the effort, the experience is
to test the lesson after you have learnt it. God tests
His Saints like chains, link by link, and therefore their
sufferings last as long as their lives. It is a shallow
creed though a very prevalent one in these days, and
hiding itself under many high-sounding names, which
says that all suffering is a bad thing, and it brings its
own righteous reward in the dilemma that God allows
so much irremediable suffering to exist.

Suffering is surely good or bad only according to

the results it produces. Had it been a bad thing in itself, the Son of God would not have taken it for His chosen instrument for the cure of the world. I do not believe there is one pang in the innumerable woes of man which has not done some good ; for suffering is effort, and every effort finds its reward. I do not mean by this that we should lessen our attempts to alleviate pain and remove the causes of distress, for such is the simple duty of charity ; I only mean that what we cannot remove is not wasted.

This then is the preparation all must undergo who would scale the heights of prayer. It may come in many forms, through trials and tribulations and heavy crosses in our external daily life ; or through the more terrible darkness and agonies of our interior spiritual life. For I have noted that the two do not, as a rule, go together, and that the soul which has exterior suffering is generally free from interior trials. Whatever the form, it will always be fruitful suffering, fruitful in the growth of virtues or the extension of influence. Further, I believe that this special suffering or preparation will only come to those who deliberately surrender themselves ; to those who know the obstacles which prevent them from attaining to God, and who, being filled with a great determination, pray that they may be purged of all that hinders, however painful the process.

Are there many, think you, who thus seek it ? Ah, so *few* compared to the multitudes on whom the light of God's Love has shone ; and yet these few are in truth a noble company. I see them, scattered though they be over the face of the world, yet gathered into one by the union of their purpose. Poor weak trembling men and women, a forlorn hope, a desperate band, pressing ever forward, reckless with longing in the face of fearful obstacles, careless of life, and consumed with desire, despised of the world and rejected of men. Above them, and around them, blazes the ceaseless fire of the Love of God, as they pass to victory—and the cross.

And now the time has come to ask what *is* this height of prayer, for which men will joyfully undergo so much, really like, when it is reached? It is quite easy to define it for it is the perfect realization, by union, of God. But when we pass from definition to description, then our difficulty begins. It is not hard to see why there should be a difficulty, for we are talking of something which happens in the depths of the soul. It is not a thing which can be apprehended by any bodily senses, or by any powers of the intellect, for it is only understood by the senses of the soul, and communicated by them in some inexplicable way to the mind.

I often think that the pages on which the Saints have tried to write a description of the heights of prayer must be blotted by many tears. They sit down to write, filled with the inextinguishable fervour which the bare memory of their experience rouses; feverishly they search for words, and at the end, reading what they have written, weep over the poverty of their failure. It needs indeed an Angel's tongue to describe that prayer, which has been named *Mors Angelorum*; for this prayer is nothing else but the bathing of the soul in God, the immersing of our being in that Love which is God : and it is unutterable. All who have experienced it have become tongue-tied, looking for words and looking in vain. If you examine the matter you will find that nearly all who have attained it end in despair by speaking of it as a fire. For it is consuming and spreading and white-hot with the infinite purity of an im-measurable heat. It is the infinite degree of anything the soul has hitherto dreamt of, and like white-hot fire it is very quiet and still, for its silence is the peace of God.

And this degree of prayer is like fire also in that it destroys. I suppose that no soul attains to a full and absolutely complete knowledge of itself until it enters into this perfect realization of God. As a fire casts forth as cinder and waste clinker all that it cannot turn into white heat, so this prayer destroys all that it cannot use. It is in truth the greater absolution. All the self that was left untouched by the preparation of suffering, the deep instincts of spiritual pride so deep as to be sub-conscious, the self-reliance so hidden as to be unknown, the self-consciousness so vague as to be indefinable ; all these are cast forth into that rubbish heap on which the cross is planted.

Nor is this the only effect of this entry into the infinite Love of God, for its chief result is that it leaves the soul able to look only in one direction—to God.

It leaves no room for other attractions, for they are blotted out. None who have ever known this degree of prayer have wondered at the phrase in the second commandment : " For I the Lord thy God am a jealous God " ; for they know that it is not possible to know infinite Love save as the sole and only Love of life, including all lesser loves in Himself.

You might think that the blotting out of attractions by this height of prayer would destroy the daily life in the world of those who know it, since it is so absorbing. But I think that the result of it is to glorify daily life with the glow of Heaven, transforming it rather than destroying it. A bar of iron cast into a red furnace itself becomes red hot, and seems to be one with the furnace and it is indistinguishable from it, but if it is withdrawn for a moment it is found to retain its former shape and character. So daily life, immersed by this degree of prayer in the Infinite Love, becomes one with it, and yet can still retain its character and individuality although it is filled with a new glory.

Thus, then, if it be God's Will, I would with poor futile words picture the soul passing on its way to God through the circle of prayer. It is no easy way, save for those who are content to loiter, but the great souls cannot afford to wait ; hunted by desire and haunted by sin, they push on with ceaseless effort. Trained by a hard discipline and cut by many a bitter experience, still panting upwards they climb the hill whereon three crosses stand.

And, when they think that all is lost and that there is nothing left to do save to lie down and die in the darkness, the Great Hand of God catches them up in Its grasp. Then as the mist of words, and the confusion of thought, clear before their eyes, they see the Divine Love, seated on a throne, crowned with thorns, which have blossomed into roses ; and as they gaze entranced upon Him, changing from glory into glory, they themselves are changed with Him, till they pass through Him into the white-hot purity of Infinite Love and are lost in God.

(ii) INTERCESSION

The Theory

WHILE it is true that during the period of our lifetime there has never been so much interest displayed in the question of prayer as at the present time, it is also true that that interest has concentrated on the subject of intercession much more than on any other part of prayer. The nature of this interest in intercession can best be seen in those questions which sum up the popular thoughts and problems concerning this kind of prayer. In some form or another, one or all of these questions will emerge in any discussion on the subject : " Will intercession make God alter His purpose? "   " Is intercession necessary at all in the case of a loving God ? " " Does intercession work by suggestion ? "

As is so often the case in any religious argument, those who pose questions at the same time unconsciously limit the freedom of answering them. Behind their questions, without recognizing it, they have already laid down certain axioms which prevent any true solution of the difficulty. In these three questions there is implicit a fundamental misunderstanding of the clear teaching of Holy Scripture on the subject of intercession. In all the questions it is taken for granted before the question is put, that intercession is an activity confined to, and dependent on, man alone. The teaching of the Bible is that intercession is never made by human beings alone and unaided. It is an activity which is always carried out in co-operation with God. We are told that the Son of God ever liveth to make intercession for us.

We are told that the Holy Ghost maketh intercession for us with groanings which cannot be uttered. We are taught that our Father in heaven knows what things we have need of before we ask Him, and therefore in His love desires that we should have them. Any theory of intercession which regards it as an activity which is confined to man is doomed to face insuperable difficulties, because it starts from a false foundation.

The true theory of intercession must begin with the axiom that this spiritual activity is something in God which is communicated to, and shared in by, man. If we take this axiom as our starting-point and seek the origin of intercession in the knowledge of God, which we have been given, we shall inevitably be drawn to consider the mystery of the Trinity in Unity. Two of the great doctrines taught by the Church concerning this mystery of the Godhead may be defined as follows : In the divine nature there are three eternal distinctions, unlike anything known on earth : these three eternal distinctions, however distinct they may be, flow into each other and exist in each other. The reason why that which is eternally distinct can and does flow into, and exist in, what is distinct from it, is to be found in the nature of God, which is Love. The eternal distinctions in the Godhead are so united and drawn together by the stream of love and desire which flows through the Godhead that they are one God. Now, when we remember that from all eternity the Incarnation was a part of the divine plan, it becomes clear that in this ever-flowing stream of love and desire which is in the Godhead our world has its place. The stream of God's desire, as it were, flows through the world in its course. Intercession on earth represents the entry of man into the stream of

God's desire. Man does not originate intercession, he joins in it.

The casual passenger, standing on the deck of a liner which is passing through the midst of a fishing fleet, notes the ocean dotted with red sails, and watches the scene of activity: the nets being drawn in, the busy sailors, and the heaps of shining fish. He turns to his companion and says, " The fishermen have caught a lot of fish to-day." To his eyes the only important element in the scene he sees is the fisherman. Yet, in reality, the fisherman is only one, and by far the most insignificant, of all the factors which have brought the fish into the boat. The wind, the tide, the warm currents in the sea, all of them mighty and irresistible forces, have had most to do with the result. The fisherman has only co-operated with them. But although his share was so small, it was most necessary. And this may serve as a picture of the work of intercession. It is the unseen, unknown, part of intercession which makes our part both possible and important. It is the wind of the Holy Ghost blowing through us, it is the tide of God's Providence, it is the current of the divine desire which really accomplish the work of intercession ; and yet the human agent is essential for the accomplishment of the activity. Intercession is the expression of God's love and desire which He has deigned to share with man, and in which He uses man.

If once we have understood, as far as human intelligence can, the source and origin of intercession, we shall be able to find a method of using this form of prayer which will be both more easy and more useful than other methods, because it will be in accordance with the real nature of intercession.

In any such method there will be three requisites corresponding to the three great marks of that stream of love and desire in God which is the source of all intercessory prayer.

The first and supreme mark of the love and desire in God is its concentration on the accomplishment of the divine will and purpose. For this reason the first place in any method of intercession must be given to worship. We are confirmed in this view by the examination of the Lord's Prayer. We note in that prayer the subsidiary place occupied by human needs. It represents the truest form of intercession, because it prefaces any attempt to put forward the needs of humanity by an effort to enter the stream of God's love and desire. The hallowing of God's Name, the desire for the coming of His Kingdom and the accomplishment of His will are recognized, and fixed for ever, as the best means of approach to intercession. Any method of intercessory prayer which has for its starting-point a list of names or needs is certain to present grave difficulties, because it is not in accord with the real nature of the spiritual activity which it is trying to carry out.

If, therefore, we are trying to draw up a method of intercession, we must begin by some form of worship. We must try to step into the great stream of love and desire, which is forever flowing through this world, before we can draw others into it. The reason so many people have felt that Holy Communion was the best and easiest time for intercession is because, in that Sacrament, our prayers for others will always be associated with worship.

The second great mark which pervades the tide which flows within the Godhead is love. The whole of the divine purpose is governed by love. There would be no connection betwixt worship and intercession if God were not love. It is because God is forever drawing every human soul to Himself by this force that it is possible for us to intercede, to draw human beings and their needs into His presence. The love of God for the world and each soul in it means that in the Godhead there is a supreme and complete knowledge of the needs of each individual. It is God's absolute understanding of each human being, in combination with the absolute desire formed by His love for their perfection, which directs the divine will and purpose. In praying for others we are made instruments to express that purpose.

As love is the most beautiful thing which exists, it must ever be in the nature of love to desire to see itself. The love of God must through all eternity desire to see its own reflection. When we intercede, this quality in divine love is in some tiny measure satisfied. Our intercessions reflect before God, in however distant a degree, something of His own infinite understanding and desire towards human beings. As the priest, standing before the polished metal ornaments of the altar, sees tiny pictures of himself in their surfaces, so our great High Priest finds His reflection in every intercessor on earth ; and, by the copying of the example of His love and sympathy, is worshipped.

But, in order that this may be so, our method of intercession must approach the work in the same spirit as His. The complete understanding, of God, the absolute desire, of His love must be reflected, even though it be faintly, in the intercessor. The second requisite of intercession is sympathy. It is evident that for most of us it is much easier to get sympathy with individuals than with movements or masses. There are, no doubt, causes with which we are so connected, and of which our knowledge is so extensive, that we can fully sympathize with them, but they are not many. Our list of intercessions must therefore be, for the most part, a list of individuals. It is requisite that in drawing these individuals into the stream of God's desire, we should understand their needs and see through their eyes.

If it is God's understanding of human needs which is the current of the stream of intercession, it is clear that our part is to be the instruments on earth which express His purpose. In order to express God's desire we must, as far as we can, share His desire, and therefore we must have the deepest sympathy for, and understanding of, those for whom we pray. It is sometimes difficult to attain to this, and it is on such occasions that the use of certain passages of Scripture are a help. Before praying for those who have injured us it is useful to read the parable of the unmerciful servant. When we desire to pray for those whose opinions or lives are alien to us, the words from the Cross will assist us. In praying for sinners, the account of the vigil in Gethsemane is a stimulus.

The third mark of the stream of the divine desire is its effort. " The Spirit itself maketh intercession for us with groanings which cannot be uttered." The mystery of effort in the Godhead is beyond human ken. We may dimly guess that the force whereby the three eternal distinctions perpetually flow into, and exist in, each other must be a tremendous and eternal activity ; the shadow of which is represented in this world by effort.

If we are to co-operate with God in intercession, if we are, in some sort, to represent on earth what He is doing in heaven, there must be an element of effort in our intercessions. The most obvious form this effort will take is that of attention and concentration. If it is hard to ensure these in other forms of prayer, it is doubly hard to do so in intercession. Each person for whom we pray offers a suggestion for wandering thoughts. In our need we shall find a powerful help in the thought of God's desire, fixed, steadfast, and constant. It is that desire which we have to join.

It is here that the value of the list appears. A list of intercessions offers some material assistance to the fixing of our thoughts, and the appointed task it represents aids us in making our effort steady. A further effort is required on our part if we are to share in God's love. It is all too easy to be apathetic in intercession, to make no real attempt, beyond a sense of duty, to really love those for whom we pray. We follow a pernicious habit of the world in using substitutes for the real thing. To love those for whom we are praying means that we must arouse our interest in them and find fresh lines of approach to them. For this reason we must prevent our intercessions from getting into a rut ; we must never be satisfied to go on repeating the same formula again and again, but rather try to discover fresh needs in those for whom we pray. In that method of intercession which requires the greatest effort, however, the making of petitions gives way to the attempt to hold the person for whom we pray in the stream of God's desire. Both methods have their place in intercession, but the second is the more satisfying of the two.

There is another way of using effort in intercession. If by some act of self-denial we can show our earnestness to God, we join ourselves to the energy of His desire.

It is not a matter of imposing any artificial form of
suffering upon ourselves, for such a course of action
has many spiritual dangers. It is rather the giving up
of some small and lawful pleasure or luxury as a sign of
the intensity of our wish that God's purpose may be
accomplished in the person for whom we are praying.

All questions concerning our intercessions are therefore seen to depend in reality on the origin and source
of that spiritual activity. The more we are able to
co-operate with the actual stream of desire in the Godhead, the easier we shall find it to intercede. It is for
us so to shape the method of our intercessions that we
accomplish this.

The Practice

An old missal preserved in a little church in Germany, contains a curious illuminated picture of Christ holding in His Hands a staff or rod of the same height as Himself, and underneath it is written, " The exact height of the Saviour of mankind when He was in the world was twelve times the height of this rod." It is very interesting to trace back this measurement to its origin, but it will suffice here to say that it can be at last connected with a golden image of our Lord set up outside the gate of the Byzantine Emperor's palace in Constantinople, which image was said to have been made in Palestine under the instruction of those who knew our Lord on earth.

My purpose in mentioning it is to use it as an illustration of how a picture, a miniature, can, nevertheless, be an exact copy of an original ; even though it be so small in its degree. For our intercession is, in its small degree, as exact a copy of Christ's intercession in this last great prayer as the picture in the missal is of the image. In order that you may appreciate this, I want you to observe certain features in Christ's intercession.

We are struck at first by the fact that all the way through His prayer He regards Himself as the channel through which God will communicate Himself to the disciples. " I have manifested Thy Name unto the men which Thou gavest Me," and again, " I have given unto them Thy words which Thou gavest Me," and " I have given them Thy word." He sees Himself in His prayer as the door through which the Sunlight of the Godhead pours into the dark rooms of the world.

The next point we note is that He demands only spiritual benefits, and not material ones for those whom He loves. " Sanctify them through Thy truth," He says, and again He prays that they may be made perfect in one, and yet again He asks that they may be with Him and behold His glory. Surely He must have foreseen that in those trials and tribulations which He had prophesied for them, His disciples would often be in need of material necessities and comforts, and yet He seeks only spiritual gifts for them.

And lastly, we can see running through the prayer a plan and order, first He seeks God's glory and the accomplishment of His work. " And now, O Father, glorify Me with Thine Own self," and then He prays for His disciples : " I pray for them, I pray not for the world," and lastly for the wide circle of the Church, " Neither pray I for these alone." It therefore remains to see how in our intercession we may copy these features.

Have you ever thought out a theory of intercession ? If you have tried to do so you must have come across a dilemma at the very outset. Why need we pray for other people ? God is their Father as He is ours, can He not give them what they need, and, if so, what use are our prayers for them ? The only possible answer to this dilemma is the true one. You cannot explain inter-cession except on the principle that God needs our co-operation to accomplish His work. We are driven at last to see that in that Divine Humanity, of which the Incarnation is the evidence to all ages, He does condescend to use our prayer as a necessary tool for carrying out His Will.

I know no thought which can add more to the dignity

of prayer than this, for by it we realize that we are indeed fellow labourers with God. I seem to see the desire of God in the likeness of a cloud of glory over-shadowing us, and requiring ever some channel by which it may be connected with every soul. Of such channels there are many and well-known ones, but the greatest in number are the intercessions we offer, which provide the means by which God's love is poured into souls. And what a condescension this is in the majesty of God that He should stoop down to the gutter where our souls lie, and use the poor straws we call inter-cessions through which to pour the mighty and healing streams of His help. If only our eyes were opened to see this process and how continually it is going on we should be amazed.

The early Christians were nicknamed by their heathen neighbours " the crickets of the night," for their psalms and hymns were heard late at night. All around us are sleepless watchers from whom a stream of inter-cession rises day and night. Many is the changed life, the sorrow lifted, the tribulation turned into joy: amazing to those to whom it has happened ! But it is not amazing to God Who has heard the stream of intercession sent up by some poor sleepless mortal lying on a bed of sickness, supposed by those around to be helpless and powerless, and yet being the means whereby a life is changed and a miracle worked. And if we learn the power of intercession we learn also its importance. Scattered over this country and over the wide world there are to be found souls waiting for the connecting link of your prayers. Will you let them wait in vain ? Will you let souls wait outside while you neglect to pray ? There is no soul who ever omitted intercession from daily prayer who has not been a source of injury to other souls.

If our Lord showed clearly in His prayer the purpose of intercession, He showed equally clearly its manner. It is almost startling to see the way in which He avoids any suggestion of praying for material needs, even when it would seem most natural. He asks for spiritual benefits for His disciples. " Holy Father," He says, " keep through Thine Own Name, those whom Thou hast given Me," but He immediately adds, as defining the purpose of this keeping, " that they may be one, as We are."

What is the meaning of this avoidance of material intercession ? Is it not that our Lord sees clearly to the root of all intercession ? And thus seeing, knows that what we really desire for other souls is not this or that earthly benefit, but " the best," that is the real and lasting satisfaction of all their desires. We cannot tie down our intercessions to seeking this or that particular benefit, for we are not sure that it is " the best " for those for whom we pray. We know by bitter experience that the material things we have desired and sought for so earnestly have often proved to be anything but " the best."

As we grow to see this more and more clearly, we feel there is only one thing we want to ask for other souls, and that is that the Will of God may be accomplished. That is the keynote of Christ's intercession.

Yet this prayer does not quite satisfy our longing to obtain special and definite blessings for others. Therefore, let us examine the prayer, and see what petitions it includes.

We desire to pray that the Will of God may be accomplished in such and such a person, or this or that society, or piece of work. What is the Will of God? Surely it is that every soul may be brought more and more into the perfect likeness of our Lord Jesus Christ till it is made one with Him. And what is this perfect likeness? It is the forming of the character of Christ in each soul. Now we know what that character was, and how in Him was perfect charity, perfect humility, perfect purity, the perfect annihilation of self-love, perfect patience, and perfect trust. For all these things, then, and for all that was in Him, we can pray.

We probably know, and that without any criticism of others, if we have learnt to know ourselves, in what qualities those for whom we pray are most deficient. Let us ask, then, that these may be given them. Or if they are in special circumstances of trouble or happiness, we can pray that such may cultivate in them special qualities. For what benefit is it to them if we pray for their material welfare? Material benefits can never make them happy, for the secret of happiness lies within. Nor can material benefits help or hinder finally their progress to the one end of their existence, which is to enter into God. In this manner, we have variety of intercession with unity of purpose.

The third feature of our Lord's intercession was its order and method. Here we touch upon a matter which is all too lightly considered by the mass of Christians; they do not seem to see that the absence of all organization, which would play havoc with their lives, will also play havoc with their prayers. We should be ashamed not to set aside a right proportion of our money for God and others. Why should we be less ashamed if we do not give a right proportion of our intercession for others?

Further, as we should not deal lightly with our money, we have no right to deal lightly with our intercession, by promising rashly to pray for all sorts of things which happen to be presented to our notice.

I cannot leave the subject of Intercession without speaking of the highest form or degree of this part of prayer ; yet the difficulty of making it clear is so great that one is tempted to give up the attempt in despair, and can only continue in the faith that God will use poor, useless words, even when they seem to fail.

However much we pray in our own power, our prayers will always be limited, for our minds and wills are bounded by mortal limits, and they set a barrier to our utmost endeavour. But if only we could be made an instrument for intercession, to be used by a power other than our own, truly then there would be no limit to our intercession. Just think, if for a moment all distracting effort were to cease and the soul were to be taken possession of by the power of God, what possibilities could be opened to prayer. If instead of our feeble efforts on behalf of others the infinite energy of God were to intercede for them, what results might there not be ? We know not what we should pray for as we ought ; but if the Spirit itself maketh intercession for us and through us, then indeed our prayers will accomplish the perfect will of God.

So those who desire to reach the highest degree of intercession must become instruments or shafts through which the intercession of God the Holy Spirit may flow into the majesty of the Godhead. Of the manner of this form of intercession it is very hard to speak, for it is only understood by experience, and the experience does not come to all souls. Have you ever in prayer for another felt the Presence of God growing closer and closer, and then striven to hold the soul you were praying for betwixt yourself and God, and as you thus held it have you felt that some great force was using you to push that soul into God? If this experience has come to you, however poorly the words may describe it, you have known this form of intercession.

And it is well to note that in this way of intercession the soul who desires to intercede is *used*. It is not passive, but it feels that its own forces are seized and united with a greater and irresistible force. By means of this manner of prayer great miracles have been and are still wrought. It is a slight miracle that one should be healed of a bodily disease, but it is a great miracle that a whole character and life should be changed and new powers given to an impotent soul : yet this miracle is often brought to pass by this high degree of intercession. Oh, if we were but awake to the tremendous powers which lie dormant in our souls for want of the life which will let them loose from their slumber, we should be able quickly to transform this world of ours with all its misery and suffering. It is sad, it is very sad, to see souls turn away from the effort needed to change their lives, when we know that the world is crying out for their help, and that such help as they have never dreamed of is locked within themselves, waiting to be used if they only will.

The great and noble band of angels who stand before the throne of the most high God, eager to do His bidding, must look with covetous eyes on us, seeing within us the possibilities of being agents meet for God's use in intercession.

I beseech you, therefore, to use th..t gift which is within you, and to remember that not for yourselves alone have you been made the Temples of God the Holy Ghost; but that through you, and with your willing co-operation, God might draw all souls unto Himself and satisfy the infinite longing of His Divine Love.

(iii) HINDRANCES AND HELPS IN PRAYER

The Variations of Prayer

OUR Lord was in His preaching continually insisting on the importance of life within form.

He was on earth the Prophet in a valley of dry bones, continually filling with life the forms He found around Him.

Ceremonial, without meaning or life, was abhorrent to Him, and He would perpetually expose it, or else fill it with a new life ; as when He stood beneath the great candlesticks in the Temple, at the moment of their ceremonial lighting, and cried aloud : " I am the Light of the World." He knew well that form was necessary for the manifestation of life, that bread and wine were necessary parts of communion : but forms must have a meaning, an inner life. So also when He laid down any form, it was always full of inner meaning ; not the least among the examples of this, is the form He laid down for private prayer, when He was instructing His disciples. We need to see the meaning which lay behind the form and, in seeing it, we shall see some of the great hindrances and helps we have in prayer.

" When thou prayest, enter into thy closet," He said. He is picturing a man turning from the outside world, leaving the talk of the market-place, the pleasure of home life, and the interests of his daily work, and going into that little dark chamber, which we call the soul. The man has left outside a great deal that he loved, and a great deal that he valued, and much that seemed to him of surpassing interest. It is this failure

in detachment which is the greatest hindrance that many
souls find in prayer. They do not wish to leave behind
so many things of which they think so much, in order
to come nearer to God. It is, they feel, a heavy price
which God requires. They are right. In order to come
nearer to God, to make progress in prayer, every soul
must pay a heavy price. If this generation is more
blind to one truth than to another, it is to the truth that
in the spiritual life all progress means paying a heavy
price. Believe me that whatever preachers at street
corners may say, religion is not an easy thing, but a very
hard one.

Now the price of progress in prayer is leaving everything which hinders. Not only everything which is
wrong (for we are all bound to do that), but everything
which hinders, which prevents us having the full and
free use of our powers in prayer. And many souls will
not face paying this price. " These things are not
wrong," they say, and they say truly, but nevertheless
they have to be left if you want to go forward in prayer.
It is, of course, a free choice which is put to you. You
can keep all these things, for there is nothing wrong in
them, but you cannot both keep them and have progress
in prayer. If you want God enough to go forward in
prayer, you must not want anything else as much as
you want Him : therefore you must be prepared to
give up many things you do want. Let us try to get
away from our conventional views about religion and
those terrible set phrases, which are so readily accepted
and so rarely thought out. Let us see our search for
God as it really is, as a high adventure, a great romance,
a desperate choice, which needs immense courage, and
wherein all progress demands a heavy price.

The next obvious hindrance to progress in prayer is distraction, or the wandering of our thoughts when we pray. "Shut the door," says Christ. He pictures the noise of the streets, the hum of conversation, and the stir of a household, filtering into the dark chamber of the soul, and the man resolutely shutting the door, that there may be silence within.

There is not one of us who does not suffer from the persecution of wandering thoughts. We kneel down to pray, and instantly the very thing we are praying about breeds a whole host of connected ideas, until we find ourselves far from our prayer. Nor is it unnatural that we should be continually harassed by such a swarm of "little gnats," as S. Teresa calls them, for they are the product of the great law of association of ideas, which governs our mind. For many a long year we have practised concentrating our minds on the things of this world, and on all that is material, and have given but a few short hours to concentrating them on God and the things of God, and so we have no cause to cry out at the result. The only cure is to do the work we have left undone ; to strengthen by long practice the power we have allowed to atrophy. Remember, wandering thoughts are not sin, but they easily can become sin. If in the midst of your prayer you suddenly become conscious that your thoughts have wandered, you are not guilty of sin ; but if, having become conscious of this, you persist in following up the train of thought, then it is sin, for you are wilfully turning your back on the God Who is calling you.

We must practise, then, in prayer, the constant recalling of our thoughts, whenever we discover they are wandering. We must resolutely shut the door each time we find it has burst open, and so in time we shall grow into the habit of concentration in prayer.

" Pray to thy Father which is in secret," says Christ. Ah! that is just the trouble. If our Father were manifest and clear, then our prayers would always be easy ; but He is in secret, and so often in the secret of darkness. I have always been less ashamed of being afraid of the dark, since I have learnt that every soul is afraid of darkness, and the night, in prayer. " There was a bitter cold wind blowing on the day they crucified Christ," says Julian of Norwich : and it has never ceased to blow at times in the soul, chilling the ardour of prayer, and numbing the faculty of the soul.

And what can possibly be the meaning of this coldness and darkness of the soul? Surely it is God's test. How should we ever grow without tests? We say to God, " I want Thee more than I can say." God replies, " Do you really want Me ? " And straightway in our prayers we find darkness and coldness, and the numbing loss of energy. If we were speaking the truth, we go on praying in spite of it ; if we were not, we stop. And if we go on praying, the darkness becomes not a hindrance, but a help : for the measure by which God values our prayers is the amount of desire in them, and it shows much greater desire to pray in darkness than in light.

For this reason it has been said that we walk faster on the way to God in darkness than in light. If you persist in prayer through darkness, you will assuredly find yourself, after the darkness has passed, much nearer to God.

We are inclined to cry out always against hindrances in prayer. Why should God let obstacles come between Himself and the soul who wants Him? I have found by experience that such a cry, whatever form it may take, comes always from one who has not penetrated very far into the spiritual life. All hindrances come either because we choose to allow them, or because they are needed to bring us nearer to God. The soul who has passed no lions by the way is not on the way which leads to the King's Palace.

In passing on to the second part of our subject we must begin by noting that all God's work is marked by its perfect adjustment of balance. Over against the degradation of humanity is set the Manger of Bethlehem; over against the sin of the world is set the Cross of Christ; over against the futility of man's effort is set the Pentecostal Tongue of Fire.

So in prayer every hindrance is balanced by a help. The price we have to pay is balanced by the desire we have to pray. We have been given a desire by God which is continually urging us on and pressing us forward. The difficulty is to use this desire by crystallizing it into some form which will strengthen and preserve it. Such a form can be found in a rule of prayer.

A rule of prayer is a written obligation by which you bind yourself to give so much time daily to God. It is the best way of beginning to pay the price. For if you set aside so much of your time, making it the first charge on each day, then you will assuredly have to give up much in order to keep it. How is this rule to be constructed? The ordinary Christian cannot do with a rule of prayer of less than an hour a day. I say this after due consideration, because so often when I have made the statement it has called forth protests.

" What! " people have said, " how can I possibly find time for an hour's prayer in my day? " Is one hour out of twenty-four too much to give to the God who made you? Will you be content to give more time to your meals than to God? What duty have you that is weightier than getting to know God? What charity has a higher claim than satisfying God's desire for you? We confine ourselves too much to principles, for people who will readily accept principles are unwilling to accept their details.

This leads me to a second help in prayer : devotional reading. As you sometimes see a dull and sullen fire turned by one poke into a bright, flaming mass, so it often happens that when a soul feels quite unable to pray, the reading of a passage from the Bible, or a spiritual work, will stir up the spirit of devotion and enable it to pray fervently. Sometimes a vocal prayer may fulfil the same purpose. Each soul knows best what part of the Bible is best for this purpose. We all know that it is not easy to find books which are a real help, and therefore I would suggest " The Hidden Life of the Soul," by Père Grou, as one of the best for this purpose. It is always more profitable to lead than to force in prayer, and a devotional book draws a soul insensibly into a state which it could not easily reach by itself.

In order that God's balance may swing true, there must be something to set against coldness and darkness in prayer. It is easy to find it, for who has not known at any rate some period of comfort and fervour in prayer? With no forewarning, very often after a period of wasted effort, we suddenly find it easy to pray. We are conscious of the nearness of our Lord. We are filled with the warmth of love, and receive a glorious consolation. Very often in our blindness we are apt to think that in some way or other we have brought about this state ourselves ; but the truth is far otherwise, for all comfort in prayer is of God's gift, it is given for a set purpose. You will find if you examine the matter that such periods of consolation always come from one of two reasons : either to revive the soul which was near to despair ; or to prepare it for a time of trial and tribulation, which lies before it. I know no more tender sign of God's Love than those periods of God's consolation. He seems to lay His Hand upon the stricken soul, filling it with divine healing and comfort ; giving it a foretaste of life in Heaven, that it may be the better able to endure life on earth. Nor do I know any greater help in prayer : for the impress left by such periods is so deep that they do not pass out of the memory ; and we are able to recall them long afterwards, in the midst of darkness and distance, and to say, " Though I be in the midst of misery and dullness, yet can I not doubt that Thou art near, for I know Thee as Thou art."

They are proofs positive that we never walk alone ; that though in the thick blackness of the night we seem to stumble forward unaided, yet by our side, unseen but exceeding close, there walks One Who, with the watchful eye of love, waits but the moment when we sink exhausted to the ground to take us in His Arms and carry us to the place where we would be.

The cry of the pilgrim of the way, " I am nothing, I have nothing, I desire nothing save the love of Jesus, and I would fain be at Jerusalem," is never allowed to rise unanswered.

Straight lies the road to God before us. It is set with
sharp stones, and it is very long, and none can travel it
without leaving much by the way, but into the hand of
the pilgrim is thrust the staff of prayer. It is beset on
every side with trials and temptations, so that none may
follow it without resolutely fixing his eyes on its end ;
but the Footprints of Him who has travelled it before
make clear the way. It descends many a dark valley,
and passes over the Hill whereon three crosses stand;
but no pilgrim travels alone, and perfect love casteth
out fear. And so at last, through many a hindrance and
many a help, the soul comes to the sight of the golden
towers and glorious spires of Jerusalem, shining in the
Light of the Sun of Righteousness.

The Body in Prayer

In the course of a recent conversation with a Quaker concerning the advantages possessed by members of the Church over members of that body, I was constrained to remark that the chief defect I could discern in the Quaker system was that, spiritually, it starved the body. It has pleased God to weld body and soul into one person : so long as that condition exists, God's gifts and God's help can never permeate the whole of a human being, unless they include some means which make the body aware of them as well as the soul. Human consciousness includes some element which is purely physical ; and, in order that the whole of our consciousness may be aware of the working of God's love, some of the means by which God communicates with us must have an outward form. A religion, which contains no sacrament, of necessity disregards the spiritual needs of one-half of the human being.

In consequence of this conversation, the problem of the connection which exists between body and soul in the spiritual life, and the respective parts which are to be played by the two partners, became a subject for thought and consideration. Nowhere can the problem be studied with greater profit than by examining the relations of body and soul in prayer ; and such an examination is all the more profitable owing to the practical maxims which may be deduced from it.

The first question which arises naturally is : What part does the body play in prayer ? It seems evident that the bodily part in prayer centres around what we call " attention." It is probable that the rules of reverence, and the mass of religious ceremonial, have all originated in the effort of human beings to fix their attention on God. Human consciousness has been likened to a perpetually flowing stream passing betwixt banks adorned with the most varied scenery. The scenery is reflected in the stream, but, at intervals, a bright beam of sunlight shining on one spot brings a reflection in the stream of unusual brilliancy. This lighted spot is attention. Our effort is to keep the position of this more vivid consciousness fixed amid the ever-moving stream. This effort, while it originates in the will, appears to be largely the work of our flesh and blood brain. The ease or difficulty of the effort varies from hour to hour with our bodily conditions. If this explanation be translated into terms of prayer, it may be said that prayer originates in desire ; but that the first step in it consists of the collection of our attention and its projection towards God. This first step is to a very large extent purely physical.

It is very suggestive to note how much of the ceremonial attached to worship has, from the earliest times, had the effect of attracting the attention of the worshippers to a central spot. The oldest adjunct to worship in the history of the world is the altar. The use of an altar is above all marked by the fact that it draws the eyes of a collection of human beings to one spot and holds them there. Further, in the evolution of religion, the figure of the priest has always emerged in witness to the fact that individual action was found to be distracting, and that there was a need to embody the action of all the individuals in one figure. The appearance of the apse and the chancel in ecclesiastical architecture may well have been a response to a deep-seated human need of concentrating attention. It is hardly surprising, in view of this, that our common experience tells us that it is much more difficult to offer private prayer in a nonconformist chapel than in a church, for in the one there is no point of concentration for the attention, and in the other there is. It is often said that people find private devotion much easier in a church where the Blessed Sacrament is reserved : very possibly this is due in part to the fact that in such a church there is a very powerful centre of attention.

It would seem from these reflections that mankind has rightly recognized the physical starting-point in prayer, and has striven to help prayer by providing assistance for the bodily part of the effort of prayer. If we judge by the analogy of our experience in the other parts of prayer, we are meant to use all such aids in order that we may learn how to train the body to accomplish always more quickly and effectively its part in prayer.

There have been two tendencies at work in organized religion, which are connected with this analysis of prayer. One of them, which is represented in its extreme form by the Quakers, is based on the fact that the activity of prayer, though it may start in the body, ends in a different sphere. This tendency has in practice aimed at eliminating the physical side of prayer as much as possible in order to reach more quickly its spiritual goal.

The second tendency, which is represented by elaborate ceremonial, has endeavoured to insure the starting-point of prayer through the bodily senses, in the belief that once prayer has started it would proceed to its natural destination. The experience of the majority of those

who have been held by mankind to be most advanced
in the art of prayer would seem to prove that the best
way lies betwixt these two tendencies. It is less helpful
to try to eliminate one part of prayer than to combine
both. The wise man will recognize that while the bodily
activity in prayer ranks below the inner and more
spiritual activity, it has nevertheless an essential part
to play in the worship of the Divine Being Who created
man a dual being.

We are therefore faced by the problem of how we
can best train our bodies to take their proper part in
prayer. The work of the body is to secure concentration, to gather up and fix attention on God. It is to be
noted that, as in every other bodily activity, habit has
a large place in the accomplishment of this. The body
learns to carry out any part of its work well and quickly
by constant repetition. I think this is one reason why
it is, in some measure, more difficult for our generation
to pray than it was for those who lived in the middle
ages. We make far more frequent and diverse calls
on our bodies for concentration than they did, and
therefore divide our energy into smaller portions.
Nevertheless, repetition of effort still remains a sovereign
remedy ; for each repetition of an action tends to lessen
the amount of initial energy required.

The first necessity in the training of the body to pray,
is the rule of prayer. By this means we obtain a regular
repetition of the effort of concentration. A road is
cut and metalled in the brain along which energy can
travel with less waste. The person who only prays
occasionally has to expend most of the energy at his
disposal on the initial and preparatory work of fixing
his attention. Such prayers are apt to be very short,

because there is no reserve of power left for the continuance of prayer.

But the regular recurrence of a time of prayer, while it is a great help, is not of itself sufficient to procure attention. Within the habit of giving time, there has to be built up a habit of using time. It is a great mistake to rush into prayer ; the recognition of the fact that some portion of the allotted time must be set apart for preparation is of the first importance for those who would avoid drifting into vagueness.

The second necessity in the training of the body to pray is the provision of a point, or points, on which attention can be concentrated. By general consent, attention in prayer is to be fixed on God. But God is infinite, and the body is finite. For bodily attention a limited point is required. When the body has done its part, the soul of man, endowed with wonderful gifts, may contemplate the infinite : but the starting-point must always be finite. The exercise most fitted to form the habit of reaching out to this transition is to be found in meditation. In this the attention is concentrated on a text or a passage, and when it is fixed, the soul is allowed to go free in its search for God.

There are many different ways in which the senses are enabled to form the habit of fixing the attention. In some cases the use of an imaginary or real picture, a crucifix, or a vocal prayer, are found to attain the end in view. In the services of the Church some central prayer, or act, or object, provide a gathering point for concentration. The aim of all preparation for prayer should be the discovery of a series of centres for attention, which will in succession stimulate the physical activities in prayer.

It must be recognized that this assistance to the body, if it is carried to extremes, falls into a danger which may make it a hindrance instead of a help to prayer. Too many points of concentration simply lead to distraction. Very ornate services are apt to bewilder the brain, and a succession of symbols disperse rather than gather our thoughts. In like manner too elaborate a programme of prayer, or the use of long lists of intercessions, soon lead to the weariness of dissipated energy. There must be a great difference in individual experience, owing to the great diversity in training and gifts : for the normal individual it would seem that in any period of prayer three points of concentration are sufficient. Many would prefer less.

But these points must be chosen and studied with care. Experience and individual preference will count for much in their choice. Points of concentration get worn out with use, and new ones have to be substituted. The orientation of spiritual interest which changes from time to time must be followed. The inner experiences of the soul, or interior messages, provide, for the period following them, the ideal centre of attention. The interests of daily life or work are not usually helpful points of concentration, and should be avoided. The posture of the body and the use of devotional gestures have their place in assisting the starting of prayer, but their value is rather transitory. In all these matters, those who desire to pray will find a fitting subject for thought and consideration.

It must be evident to all who have seriously reflected on this matter, that it brings into view a difficult, and even terrible, problem. Since the body has this important part to play in prayer, what is to happen when illness or infirmity makes it impossible for the body to give its contribution ? Is prayer dependent on bodily health ? The answer to this question is not easy. The greater part of prayer is dependent on the soul, but the form of prayer is to a large extent dependent on the body. The pious books of my childhood always insinuated that a bed of sickness was an ideal place for prayer. That is an exploded theory. Our common experience teaches us that, although a bed of sickness can be, and often is, a place of great spiritual happiness and welfare, it is one of the worst places in the world for the practice of prayer in the form to which we are accustomed.

It is unfortunate from our point of view that the first of all our powers to suffer from bodily ill-health is concentration. It begins to fail before any physical signs of disease appear. It is usually the last of our qualities to recover. After an operation, when the doctor has declared that our body is restored to health, a further period must pass before we are capable of any sustained attention. It must also be remembered that a greater degree of concentration is usually required for prayer than would be required for reading a heavy book. This provides a rough and ready test for measuring our responsibility for attention in prayer. If during any period of prayer we could have read with profit a solid book on some subject which interested us, we may be sure that we ought to have been able to make the effort required for concentration in our prayer.

In view of these facts, it might seem that prayer during illness must be dismissed as a hopeless task. Such is not the case, because there is fortunately one form of prayer which is immune from bodily obstruction. This form is termed ejaculatory prayer. It is a prayer which consists of short sentences or ejaculations of momentary duration. It requires the very smallest amount of attention or concentration. It is particularly suitable to times of illness or worry, because pain or anxiety automatically suggest it and remind us of it. It is of great spiritual value, because it insures a very frequent recollection of God, which greatly strengthens the soul. Moreover this habit of ejaculatory prayer learnt in sickness, persists afterwards in health, and so our crosses are crowned with profit.

Those who are ill will do well, if the illness is such as to prevent them from doing their daily work, to give up their rule of prayer and replace it by frequent ejaculatory prayer. As they emerge from illness the rule of prayer should be gradually replaced by taking up a small daily time of prayer, which can be increased week by week. Many people have suffered much from the fear that they had failed or sinned because they were unable to force themselves to pray during times of ill-health ; but if these simple suggestions are followed, such times may prove to have benefited the life of the soul instead of hindering it.

We cannot in religion cut out one-half of God's construction of mankind ; we must therefore take into account in all questions of prayer the needs of the body. Nevertheless we are responsible for training the body to assist and not to hinder the spiritual life. The key-stone of the Creed is the Incarnation of the Son of God, and right at the centre of Incarnation is to be found the body. It must therefore have its rightful and important place in all religion, and in our own spiritual life.

Devotional Reading

If the patron saint of Meditation is S. Bartholomew, the saintly patronage of devotional reading may be allotted to the Ethiopan chamberlain of Queen Candace. But the distinction between the two is evident. In the one case Nathaniel after prayer was reading the account of the dream of Jacob, and God revealed in it a meaning which had reference to his life and prepared him to receive the message of Christ. In the other case the Ethiopian was reading Isaiah's picture of the suffering servant, and it was the comment of a human agent which kindled in him the desire for baptism and awoke his spiritual life to a new fervour. It may be added that the rank of these two aids to the life of the soul corresponds to the rank of their patron saints, of whom one was an apostle and the other a convert.

In any useful discussion of devotional reading we must take account of its advantages and of its limitations. Few things have caused greater difficulties in the world than the theory of inspiration, which has offered a notable example of the harm wrought in life by too limited thought. It has illustrated the passionate instinct of mankind to find safety through an intellectual " trade union " policy of reducing thought to the terms of the lowest human capacity and excommunicating those who refused to confine themselves to this level. It is a feeling, common to us all, that it is so much easier to attach certainty to a word than to a process. Yet inspiration must be a process ; the in-breathing of the power and wisdom of God must be a living thing, capable of an infinite number of degrees, the resultant

of many factors, subject to the influences of time and
environment, changing and growing alike in the individual and the race, and only governed by the plan of
God and the needs of man.

The inspiration of the Bible differs from other inspiration not in nature, but in content. It is part of the same
process as all inspiration, whether in sermon, prayer,
book, or picture, but it contains more than any of them.
" Holy Scripture containeth all things necessary to
salvation." This cannot be said of any other writing ;
yet of many sermons, prayers, books, music, and pictures
it may be said, as it is said of the Bible, that they are
the result of the in-breathing of God's power and wisdom.
And herein lies the great justification of the practice of
devotional reading. It is, in fact, the use of, and co-
operation with, the great process of inspiration which
is forever going on in the world : a process whereby the
power and wisdom of God is continually flowing out
into the world to aid the growth and development of
man's soul.

The main purpose of devotional reading is to seize
and use this inspiration, to catch again the breath of
God enclosed in human words. It is just because our
own inspiration is so partial and faulty, so dependent
on many factors, that this form of reading is such a help.
This is the first and great advantage of devotional
books. They act, like the starting handle of a motor,
by drawing in some of the living power of God to enliven
our lack of life, they waken our prayer into activity.

We come to prayer in this world, surrounded by the
atmosphere of our daily life, encumbered with the
cares and thoughts of what we have done or are going
to do. The necessary change from concentration on

this world to concentration on the world of the Spirit, is facilitated by the flash of inspiration, the glimpse of God's life, conveyed through the words of the writer. All prayer, like all growth, is subject to variations of intensity. The dull period follows the bright as night follows day. Owing to this variation we stand in great need of outside helps. In times when prayer is hard and concentration is difficult the devotional book is a real aid. It strengthens our concentration and provides a means of fixing our mind on God when we cannot unaided turn it in that direction.

Another advantage is to be found in the fact that, for the most part, devotional books are the expression of experience. The writers have themselves faced the difficulties and problems of the spiritual life, very often in an acute form. They are not theorists laying down logical ideas, but practical men and women who know the real difficulties and have had to find their way through them. There is a type of devotional book of which this cannot be said, but it is comparatively rare. In such books a cast-iron system of dogmatic rules form the basis of instruction.

It is evident, when this advantage of devotional reading is considered, that there must be many occasions in the spiritual life when we can find useful guidance in the face of our own problems from the experiences of these writers. The explanation of some state of which we were aware in our own prayer, but were unable to define ; the suggestion of some exercise or method of prayer to meet the special need of the moment ; the solution of some difficulty we could not explain ; all these, in many cases, are to be found through the reading of devotional books.

A third advantage of this form of reading is to be found in its witness to continuity. Going back, as these books do, through many centuries, it is both strange and comforting to find how modern they are. They form an unique class of literature in that they are never out of date. For those who might well feel dubious because they had discovered in their lives some new and unexpected experience, they provide both proof and encouragement. They prove that the new experience has its place in the normal process of God's self-revelation to human beings ; and they encourage the fearful to go forward when they might lose their greatest opportunity by holding back.

Yet while these advantages are so great as to render this form of spiritual help almost a necessity, it must not be forgotten that there are certain limitations attached to it. Forgetfulness of these limitations deprives those who use it of many of its benefits. Inspiration is a process which requires co-operation if it is to be effectual. The in-breathing of God is enclosed in human words and will not be apprehended save by those who are in a condition which it can penetrate. This warning is all the more necessary because it is one of the extraordinary features of our lives that we are apt to take the most important things so much for granted that we forget them. The most important thing about devotional reading is the prayer which precedes it, and without which we can hardly expect that it will assist us. Yet I should not like to say how often I have forgotten this prayer and have felt afterwards that this form of reading was a very much overrated aid to the spiritual life. That vision of wisdom, of the work of the Holy Ghost, which inspired the writers of Ecclesiasticus and the Wisdom of Solomon, is an essential requisite for the profitable perusal of devotional literature. It is God the Holy Ghost who reveals, in answer to prayer, the real meaning of what we read, and restores to prosaic words the glow which filled them in the mind of their writer.

A second limitation in these books arises from the difference between their inspiration and that of Holy Writ. They are partial and not universal in their contents. And therefore each book will appeal to certain people only, or at certain times only. It is not uncommon to find the readers of these books in distress because they have never had the experiences described by their writers, or, if they have had them, they experienced them in some very different form. It cannot be stated too clearly that God deals with every human being individually. While certain processes by which He moulds us, and certain general conditions of prayer, are common to all, the difference in form, degree, and order of experience is almost infinite.

This difference is rendered more acute by the great divergence between the symbols used by different persons to express that which must be expressed by symbol. To mention two great classes only : there are those who will always use personal symbols such as Friend, Shepherd, Guide, &c. ; and there are those who will always use impersonal symbols such as Fire, Light, Sea, &c. It is clear that unless this limitation, due to the individuality of the writer is recognized, devotional reading may be the cause of great confusion. It is a mistake to approach one of these books with the idea that it must reflect as in a mirror our own lives, or our own way of approach to God. It is likely that in some points it will meet our own experience of the spiritual life ; it is certain that in others it will seem to have no connection with it.

A third limitation is due to the fact that these books deal with spiritual life, that is to say, with something which is growing and moving all the time. They are forced to fix, like a photograph, one moment in a state of motion and there must always be a certain loss of reality in doing this. In our own lives it often happens that in looking back we can fix in this manner some past process, can see a temptation or a development in a static form ; but we cannot do the same with the period in which we are living, or the spiritual experience through which we are passing. It follows that while devotional reading often clears our view of God's dealing with us in the past, it is comparatively seldom that it enables us to identify the present with the same certainty. If such a book is mainly concerned with the description of a process or condition of prayer which has not been fixed in our past, it has little meaning for us.

But in spite of these limitations there are certain features which make the classics of devotional literature universal in their appeal. A great French actor once went to hear Massillon preach and, as he came out, truth forced from his lips a confession humiliating to his profession : " My friend," he said to one of his companions, " this is a prophet, and we are only actors." There is, in spite of the tower of Babel, one universal language which all humanity can understand. It is the language of reality. Those who have had contact with God, the great reality, reveal that contact in word or tone, and it is comprehended by every human being.

The spark of reality in these books finds an answering spark in each of their readers.

Moreover, it is this quality of reality which lifts them above those age-long controversies which have been the plague of religion. These are writers for that universal Church of the Future towards which we look and to which we make our appeal. Catholic and Protestant, high and low, are terms which vanish before the serenity of their outlook ; and to them is confided the noble task of repairing the robe of Christ rent by the army of controversialists.

And in yet another point is their appeal universal. In most of us there is a very healthy revolt against dictation. Even if it be unconsciously, we resent the intrusion of a barrier which limits the freedom of our relationship to God ; we feel the difference between the suggestion which stimulates growth and the dogmatic injunction which checks it. Now all great devotional writers have one common characteristic in their humility. When they speak to us they look upwards not downwards ; it may be that sermons would have done more for the world than they have done had they been preached from a pit in the chancel instead of from the pulpit. The devotional book touches so many of us because it is written from our own level. The author places himself where we are and recognizes, before the presence of an omnipotent God, his equality with us.

It may not be amiss, in conclusion, to indicate some of the special periods in our spiritual life when special authors are most likely to prove helpful. In times of dullness and depression Brother Lawrence and Blessed Julian of Norwich are useful. In times of great darkness S. John of the Cross is a valuable guide. In normal times, when there is need of perseverance, Thomas Upham (sometime congregational minister in Massachusetts) is a sound guide. In periods when there is great progress in prayer S. Theresa, Father Baker, and Père Grou may be recommended. For those who seem to be more advanced in prayer than in a holy life, S. Francis de Sales and William Law provide a tonic. As stimulants, when prayer seems to have fallen into a rut, Richard Rolle, Walter Hilton, and Ruysbroek may be suggested.

Holy Communion

Of the Blessed Sacrament of the Body and Blood of Christ we may well say with the Patriarch Jacob, " This is none other than the Gate of Heaven," for assuredly at the consecration a door is opened into Heaven and through it comes the Lord of Love bearing His Life to men. Nevertheless this sight is not for all eyes to see, and it is with Christians at the Eucharist as it was with the blind man healed by our Lord; at first they see nothing but hear a voice; then they see but dimly " men as trees walking " ; and lastly they see the Glory that is there. Let us, therefore, set down in poor words that which happens in the Blessed Sacrament, and then the way to know it.

It is hard for us who live in this world, manifest to our senses, to know that it is a prison; that we are bound by earthly bodies in a circular prison while all round the outside of our prison is freedom and the other and true world : the world of eternal life. Nevertheless so it is, nor are there any ways by which we may escape from prison into the true life save three : prayer, the Blessed Sacrament, and death. In all these ways a soul may leave the body and pass through a door opened in the shell of the prison into the world of eternal life. In the first two ways the soul must return from its excursion, but in the third it remains. We may not compare these ways, for in order to make comparison we need to know the whole extent of each and no human being may do this. Nevertheless we may say that each in its order is more universal than the one before it.

So in the Blessed Sacrament there is opened, before each Christian, a door. Through this door our Lord Himself enters this world. I beseech you to consider this a moment. We know that our Lord is in all things our perfect example. Here daily He sets before us an example of perfect humility. In all the glory of His Ascended Majesty, the Judge of all the world comes to us, not as in Bethlehem for all the race, but for a few poor dazed and blind souls gathered together to meet Him. While they wait there, battling with distracting thoughts, cold and with little love, He lowers Himself in exquisite pity to come to their prison for love of them. Truly He does, Himself, that which He requires of us in the Day of Judgment, for we are sick and He visits us, we are in prison and He comes unto us.

Nor is this all, for He Himself brings with Him the food of life. All life is in Him, and from this overflowing store He feeds the sick prisoners, giving them life and strength for their bodies in His Body and for their souls in His Blood. It is this Eternal Life, from the world of eternal life, which keeps alive the soul of the world ; which glows and vibrates in each soul, lighting something in other souls, and feeding the spiritual life of the world. Daily is the prison of the world of our senses broken into by the victorious Lord, daily are the souls therein filled with the life which will enable them to break out of it into their true home, the world of eternal life.

It would, however, be a narrow view of this great means of grace which limited its purpose to this world of ours. For the life which proceeds from the other world is like a wave which, passing through the door, floods those who receive it, and then like a wave recedes, drawing them with it through the gate.

Many are they who know these things to be true yet long to experience them. It were well that they should remember in the first place that in general the approach to any spiritual experience is by a long and slow growth ; that, above all, long training and practice are needed. This seems to be especially true of the Blessed Sacrament : for it is usually only by slowly learning devotion and concentration, by a long desire, and by the constant frequenting of this Holy Communion that the soul comes to the experience. First comes the conviction, the certainty, that there is a Presence in the Blessed Sacrament. Then perchance the soul is aware on certain occasions of a direct message at the time of Communion and this may happen frequently. Then very dimly the Presence becomes more real, bringing a new sense of awe. While, finally, for those happy few whom God brings to this state, comes the frequent entry into the world of eternal life, the overpowering sense of the entering Lord, and the moment of blissful Communion.

There is no royal way for those who seek the full revelation of this Sacrament. It is only by patient discipline and long practice that clear sight comes. I would not speak further of details lest they should be held as more important than they are, but I append a few maxims which may assist the soul.

1. It is Desire which is the key to the door of experience.
2. True desire manifests itself in patience and perseverance.
3. Perseverance is chiefly shown in maintaining a constant standard in preparation for Holy Communion, and thanksgiving after it.
4. Distracting thoughts are not sins unless they are consciously persisted in.

5. It is as well to have certain places in the service at which the attention is always specially concentrated (e.g., Prayer for Church militant. Sanctus. Prayer of oblation) ; this serves as a safeguard against vagueness.

6. The true experience may be known by the joy and vitality it brings.

7. There is no way to prolong experience beyond the time our Lord wills, but we can remove all hindrances to its prolongation on our part by complete and constant surrender.

It is painful to write words on this subject knowing their poverty and how little they touch even the fringe of that which is in this Sacrament. Nevertheless I pray that all who read them may be aware of the open door, and of the Lord Who enters, of the life He brings, and, if it be His will, of the world from which He comes.

TRAVELLERS ON THE WAY

Sainthood

" ALL SAINTS." Those two words might well stand as the motto of the Catholic Church, a promise of the past, an ideal of the present, and a prophecy of the future. For neither the Church nor its teachers ever thought of the saints as a class, as a group separated from the rest ; they were to be the whole, and " all saints " was simply to be another name for the Church.

S. Paul, when he wrote his greeting to the Corinthians from Philippi, did not mean it to be a greeting from a section of the Christians in that city ; he meant it to be a greeting from the whole Philippian Church.

In the days after the apostles, when the Church spread through the world like the leaven through a loaf, when sincerity was harder to test, and sad experience had shown the tares among the wheat, men began to forget the teaching of the apostles and to think of the saints as a peculiar people reaching a standard beyond the powers of the ordinary man. Of late years I would fain believe there has been a return to more primitive views, and we are beginning to acknowledge that the Church expects every member to be a saint ; that Christianity has but one standard, that of sainthood, to offer to every Christian. In pursuance of this belief I would put before you, as a matter touching your life most intimately, what it means to be a saint, and what is the cost of sainthood.

It ought not to be very hard to define a saint. We have a great deal of material to draw upon, in order to find out what makes a saint. We have hundreds of men and women who, by the practically unanimous opinion of mankind, were saints. We have some, whose names are well known to everybody, who are elected, as it were, to their position by public acclamation ; such men and women as S. Francis of Assisi, S. Catherine of Siena, or S. Teresa of Spain. We have others more ancient in date and less popularly known, whose titles are acknowledged in the calendar of our Prayer Book, and of whom examples are to be found in S. Cyprian or S. Jerome.

Now what was it that made these people saints? Why were they so universally recognized as reaching the standard set before the Church? Let us examine a few episodes drawn from the life of these people, so that we may see the principle underneath the world's recognition of sainthood.

Let us first take a little fragment from the old chronicle of the life of S. Francis of Assisi. " On a day when he was praying fervently unto the Lord, answer came unto him : ' Francis, all those things that thou hast loved after the flesh thou must needs despise, and from those that aforetime thou didst loathe thou shalt drink great sweetness and delight unmeasured.' Rejoicing therefore at these words, when as he rode nigh unto Assisi, he met one that was a leper, and for that he had been wont greatly to loathe lepers, he did violence unto himself and dismounted from his horse and gave him money, kissing his hand. And receiving from him the kiss of peace, he remounted his horse and continued his journey." Now what was it in this man that drew from mankind the vote of sainthood? To what were they looking when they thought such an act a sign of holiness? By whom had the touching of lepers and the love for beggars been hallowed? In the answer to that question you will find the principle which underlies sainthood. It was because Francis was doing something that Christ had done that he became S. Francis, and the world saw in his deed a reflection of Christ's deed and canonized him.

Or take again S. Catherine of Siena; that city which was the very home of the vendetta and the blood feud, where men drew their sword at a name before they knew its owner. Picture that day when the family of the Rinaldina, returning from a wedding, entered the little Church of San Cristoforo and saw there in a group before the altar the rival house of Maconi. In an instant both parties had drawn their swords, and if the history of Siena were any guide, it was little likely that any man would leave that church unwounded. At the same moment a clear voice of authority turned every head to the altar step, where stood a woman in white: S. Catherine, whom the common people called the Lily of Christ. She bade the strong men gathered there, to give one to the other the kiss of peace. Enmity died out of their hearts; silently and sincerely they obeyed, and so passed out before the amazed crowd arm in arm, to work together for their city's good.

Why was it that the people of Siena called that woman a saint? Was it for any other reason save that they knew of only One Who had caused quarrels to cease and forbidden the fire of vengeance to be kindled, and so watching this woman they knew that she must be approximating to the example of Christ. The world, when it speaks as a whole, has a habit of speaking the truth, and the truth, which the world speaks here, is that sainthood is something in the image and likeness of Christ.

I will take but one more example, and that of a less-known one. S. Cyprian, whom the Church of England commemorates on September 26th, was a bishop of Carthage, a learned and courageous man. After a life of wonderful devotion and service to the African Church he was summoned on a day to stand his trial before the Proconsul Paternus, who charged him thus : " The most sacred Emperors Valerian and Gallien have done me the honour to send me a despatch in which they have directed that persons not following the Roman religion must conform to the Roman ceremonies or die. What answer have you to give me ? " To which Cyprian the Bishop answered : " I am a Christian and a bishop. I know no other gods but the one and true God, Who made heaven and earth. He is the God Whom alone we Christians serve." He was an old man, one who had moved in the best society of his day, who had many friends at court, who knew that just a little prevarication would save him ; and yet he chose to tell the whole truth. The Proconsul wrote on his tablet and read aloud the sentence : " Our pleasure is that Thascius Cyprianus be executed with the sword." " Thanks be to God," said Cyprian. Straightway he knelt upon the ground and prostrated himself in prayer ; then rising, he desired his friends to give the executioner twenty-five pieces of gold in token of his forgiveness: so suffered the blessed Cyprian.

What does our Church see in all this which leads it to call this man saint? Surely if there had not been One Who, before him, stood boldly before the Roman judge and pledged His life to keep faith with mankind, Who prayed for His executioners and died without a murmur, the Church would never have known that Cyprian was a saint. Take what example you like and you will always find the same truth beneath it : that the saint is a saint solely and wholly because his life approximates visibly in some particular to Christ's life ; that he is crowned with a halo because the reflection of the Light of the World has shone visibly around his head

Now you can see why the primitive idea was the true one, and why you and I are expected to be saints. What is our profession save to follow the example of our Saviour Christ and to be made like unto Him? And what is this save the profession of a saint? Ah! if we Christians only had more spiritual ambition there would be no room left vacant in the heavenly Calendar.

How comes it that saints are still looked upon as a class apart, instead of being normal examples of membership of the Church? The answer to that question is to be found in the cost of sainthood. It cannot be too often or too clearly proclaimed, that Christianity is something for which a big price has to be paid. When all around us the air is full of vague rumours of a new-found faith which is free of effort, and tolerant of everything save toil and pain, it is time to speak out boldly and to say that true Christianity is the most costly possession in the world, that it still knows but one road, which leads over Calvary, and still has but one symbol, which is a cross. If a saint is one who approximates to the life of Christ, it is self-evident that he is one who suffers in the endeavour to come to God. There were many ways in which our Lord could have saved the world, but He was limited in His choice, for God can but choose " the best," and the way He chose was the way of suffering, of hard discipline, and severe tests. The man and the woman who is not prepared to pay this price cannot attain the profession of sainthood to which they are called.

What do I mean by the suffering of the hard discipline and the severe test, in the ordinary life of an ordinary person who desires to be a saint? I mean that the cost of these things is not dependent on their appearance outwardly, but on the suffering they give inwardly. It is not necessary to be hung upon a cross in order to be crucified, an idle slander accepted meekly will do instead. It is not necessary to kiss a leper to secure self-discipline, a genuine effort to be kind and companionable to a person we dislike intensely will do as well. It is not necessary to face martyrdom before a heathen judge to secure a severe test, for the humble acceptance of a sudden insult or the true and instant forgiveness of a wrong will serve as well. The most frequent delusion of any spiritual life is, that given great opportunities it might have a chance of sainthood.

The necessary materials for the building up of a saint are in every life ; they only need to be used. Do you want to be a saint? Some very simple rules will serve your purpose. Begin by fixing the amount of time you give to prayer and keep that time as the first call on your life. Very often we should do this if it were not for our daily duties. There is nothing concerning which we have so lost our sense of proportion as our daily duties. For what duty have we which is more important than our duty towards God, and what is any other duty, save a useless waste of time, if our duty towards God, from the doing of which alone all the value of our work proceeds, is left undone? And all else is summed up in four sayings left by one of those concerning whose title to saintliness mankind has never doubted, whose works next to the Bible still have the greatest circulation. He left these four guiding words to those who followed :—

1. Desire always to do the will of another rather than thine own.

2. Choose always to have less rather than more.

3. Seek always the lowest place and to be beneath everyone.

4. Offer up thyself, that the whole will of the Father may be fulfilled in thee.

At the Holy Eucharist throughout the world there are gathered together many humble souls ; in the eyes of the world they lead perhaps grey and undistinguished lives, their sorrows and their joys, and all their opportunities seem small and of little account ; but this they have in common, that they are bent at all costs on following the example of Christ and growing in His likeness. It is to this hidden congregation, in which I pray we may have our part, that there rings down from the glorious courts of Heaven the message of good comradeship—

" All the saints salute you."

The Making of a Saint

It is, I suppose, true, that the objects with which we are most familiar are the ones which arouse least curiosity in our minds. It is, therefore, likely that most of us accept the furniture of our rooms and houses without thinking much of the processes by which it was made. Yet, if a man be interested in the art of cabinet making, each piece of furniture presents an interesting problem, and he comes to learn that all furniture goes through three main processes. First of all the wood has to be shaped, then prepared, and last of all polished. To anyone who has been engaged in carrying out one or other of these processes it must sometimes occur that the Divine Carpenter, carrying out what He had learnt in His earthly apprenticeship at Nazareth, has applied these same processes, and no other, to the making of those saints who are to adorn His heavenly kingdom, and to beautify His Church on earth.

The making of a saint is a piece of craftsmanship unequalled by any other. The skill, the long patience, and the labour it involves, make it pre-eminent in all the constructive work of God. Yet the processes by which it is accomplished are as simple and easy to define as those of the carpenter ; and our Lord laid them down in one short verse. Let us consider in turn the three steps in the making of the saint, and by taking some striking example of each of them endeavour to learn what meaning they have for our own lives, for we also are called, as S. Paul tells us, to be saints.

The first step by which the wood is prepared for its ultimate end is its shaping. It has to be cut into the pattern which will best fit it for the place it is to occupy. In like manner our Lord began His direction to His disciples by saying " Whosoever will come after Me, let him deny himself." That means to say that the training of a saint will begin by his learning to ignore, to refuse to recognize, himself. Our Lord uses the same word when He speaks of S. Peter denying all knowledge of his Master. To most of us self is a very potent master. To ignore our whims and selfish desires and self-will is one of the hardest of tasks. Yet if we do not do it we cannot be shaped by God. S. Paul recognizes the difficulty of the task and can find no term adequate to represent it except the word " death." " I am dead," he says, " that I might live unto God." But in no way, I think, can we better understand the full meaning of this word of Christ, than by taking an example and trying to see what it involves for a saint in the making.

There was once a young man, endowed with a brilliant intellect, provided with a splendid education, and gifted with a lovable character. He soon acquired a prominent position and a great reputation. Yet all his gifts were marred by self-will ; his intellect he used to gain renown ; in his pride he thought his mind capable of being the final judge of the problems of the spirit. His education he used for empty disputation and selfish gain in argument. His gift of love he debased in the mire of impurity. Yet, steadily the urging of the Holy Ghost sapped at his defences. Little by little he learnt the limitations of his intellect, more and more he became aware of the degradation of evil living. Driven from defence after defence, he felt obliged to learn instead of to teach ; to humble himself to become a pupil of the faith he had scorned ; and to repent in dust and ashes

and utter misery for his sins against morality. The self
to which he had listened, he found to be a false guide,
and turning his back on it he denied its impulses and its
mastery, and set himself to do what he would not and
to be what he could not. In his later life this young
man, whom now we know as S. Augustine, saint and
doctor of the Church, wrote as follows : " When I was
young I approached the study of the Holy Scriptures
with acuteness of disputation not with piety of enquiry,
by my moral perversity I closed the door against myself ;
I ought to have knocked at the door that it might be
opened to me, but I presumed to seek with pride what
none can find but by humility."

This then is the first process in the shaping of the
saint, and we have to ask what place it has in our own
lives. Each of us is endowed in our degree, as was
S. Augustine. Each of us is tempted to use our endow-
ment of love, or intellect, or skill, for our own selfish
ends, for our own pleasure, and our own self-will. How
great a struggle it is to deny these claims. It is not in
big things, it is in small ones that we can submit ourselves to the shaping. It is in the little thing we shall
be tempted to say to-morrow ; in the trivial plan from
which we are determined not to be turned ; in the
selfishness of our love, that the means of our shaping
are to be found. Unless in these things we will to ignore
ourselves, how can the grace of God reach us ? There is
a pregnant saying of S. Augustine we shall do well to
bear in mind—" God will bow down His ear, if thou
dost not lift up thy neck."

Next to the shaping comes the preparing of the wood.
Each piece must be levelled with the plane, smoothed
with the scraper, and rubbed down with the glass paper.

Were the wood possessed of feeling, we can imagine it would cry out in agony under these processes. Certain it is that this same stage in the making of a saint is full of pain. " Whosoever will come after Me," saith Christ, " let him take up his cross." What does that mean ? It means that those who would be saints must put themselves into the position of a condemned man ; in other words, they must be prepared to face shame and loss even in the most extreme forms. It is little wonder if you and I would like to scratch these words out of the Bible, for while we may conceive of ourselves as being ready to give up self-will that God may shape us, we can hardly picture bearing shame (particularly if we be held to deserve it) or losing what we value most.

Let us turn to the life of a saint and try to see what it means in practice. There lived in Spain a young monk ; some of the best blood of Spain ran in his veins, and with it the pride and arrogance of the noble caste, although he had been brought up in poverty. He became a Carmelite friar, distinguished for his learning and his power. But he soon discovered that the Order to which he belonged had lost its fervour. With the aid of a friend he set to work to reform the Carmelites, and met with great opposition. He did not attempt to force the reformed rule on others, but his holy and self-denying life was a reproach to the unreformed friars. One midnight they burst into his cell and dragged him off to prison. For nine months he was incarcerated in a close, dark cell, so small he could hardly move or breathe. He could not read for want of light, was fed on bread and water, and scourged thrice a week. At the end of nine months he escaped, and in time reached a high office in the reformed Carmelite Order. But soon internal dissension arose among the monks, and on charge of being in league with disloyal members of the Order, he was judged guilty and deprived of his office. Some six months after this blow, he died, holding in his hand the crucifix which he kissed repeatedly. If ever a saint were allowed to feel something of the shame and reproach of the *Via Dolorosa* it was S. John of the Cross, and yet he found in it a joy which as a poet he has beautifully expressed in this verse :—

> O burn that burns to heal!
> O more than pleasant wound,
> And O soft hand, O touch most delicate
> That dost new life reveal,
> That dost in grace abound,
> And slaying, dost from death to life translate.

It is not wonderful that there are so few saints on the calendar when we consider this stage in their making. Yet it is this which Christ calls us all, if not to undergo, at any rate, to be prepared to undergo. There may be something romantic to us in the thought of a prison or a cross, but there is nothing romantic about the cross as it comes actually in life. It is the little disgrace, the contempt of our neighbours, the loss of something we valued, which is the true cross, and the more a cross because it so often comes from our own folly or carelessness. Our first impulse is to get angry or sullen, to turn our backs on it by insincerity or self-will. Yet the way of saintliness lies in quiet, simple acceptance, bearing the burden in constant dependence on God and trusting in Him to use it somehow for His glory. You cannot be a Christian without suffering for it in some way, and your advance in the spiritual life depends on how you bear that suffering. S. John of the Cross wrote one

sentence which puts the whole matter in a nutshell
when he said, " We must not seek to adjust our trials to
ourselves, but we must adjust ourselves to our trials."

When the wood has been shaped and prepared, there
still remains one process if it is to attain its full beauty.
It is necessary to polish it by the constant repetition
of rubbing with oil or polish. In the making of the
saint, this process is represented by the last clause of
Christ's sentence, " Whosoever will come after Me, let
him follow Me." That means that we have got to
persevere in the exacting course of a personal following
of Christ's example, a following which will be both
habitual and permanent. I am inclined to think this
process is really harder than either of the other two.

We know by experience what changeable creatures
we are, how different we feel to-morrow from what we
feel to-day. Yet it can be done, and to prove it to you
I would call your attention to one of the noblest English-
men on the calendar of saints. His parents must have
had some foresight of what he was to be, for they called
him by a name which meant prayer. While a child he
was sent to a monastery to be educated ; the twenty
monks who formed the community died from a cruel
epidemic, which left only this child and the abbot alive.
The two continued as they best could to celebrate the
entire canonical services, with obstinate precision, until
new brethren joined them.   The child grew up and was
ordained, and passed all the rest of his life in the
monastery, dedicating his whole time to study and
meditation on Holy Scripture : without other pleasure,
as he himself said, than to learn, to teach, to write, and
to pray! His days and nights, of which a very moderate
portion was given to sleep, were divided between his

prayers and studies, and the instructions which he gave
to some six hundred monks. The laborious severity of
his life in the cloister did not hinder an extensive and
important intercourse with the world outside. In spite
of criticism and a cruel accusation of heresy, he continued in gentleness and patience his unremitting labour.
His end was as his life, for as he approached his last
breath, the young monk to whom he dictated his last
work, said to him, " Beloved Master, there remains only
one verse which is not written." " Write it then,
quickly," said the saint. A moment later the monk told
him, " Now it is finished." " You say truly it is
finished," replied the saint. Then lying on the floor
of his cell he sang for the last time, " Glory be to the
Father, to the Son, and to the Holy Spirit," and as he
pronounced the last of the divine names he gave up the
ghost. Such is the perseverance which our Master calls
us to give, a perseverance which implies a constant
struggle. The Venerable Bede, whom we have just
been considering, summed it up when he taught his
pupils this saying, " In the Resurrection, no doubt,
everything shall be perfected. In the meantime, it is
a great thing to keep the field, and remain unconquered,
though not discharged from war."

Of all the tests of the saint I suppose this is the hardest
for us. To go on day by day without getting slack,
without continual stimulus, is an awful task. Look back
on life and you will see how often we have had the
opportunities of sainthood, and how often we have lost
them because we would not persevere. Yet this is
certain, that there is no moment too late in life to begin
the making of a saint ; that if now we set ourselves to
ignore self-will, to face humiliation and contempt, and

to persevere steadfastly, the way lies open which leads
to the very throne of God.

I do not know what you feel as you contemplate the
lives of these men whom God shaped into saints here on
earth, but in my mind is left a great thankfulness that
God through them should have glorified Himself. I
can conceive of no tribute from all the choir of angels,
which has so exalted His Name and honoured His
majesty, as the lives of these men shaped by Him. If
I am not, through my sins and faithlessness, like them,
I can, at any rate, rejoice with Him that they have lived
to His glory : I can pray and desire that you and I
may add, if not a ray to His splendour, at any rate, one
little speck which will glitter in the light of His love,
making it the more visible to all men.

The Work of a Saint

S. Matthew x. 5.
" These twelve Jesus sent forth."

That was an adventure, if you like. If you consider any modern adventures, such as going to the North Pole or going to a war, and then compare such a task with the Apostles' task, and such an equipment with the Apostles' equipment, you will understand what a hare-brained scheme it must have looked at the time. To discover a certain spot in a field of ice, or to fight a battle, is such a tiny piece of work when you compare it with the work of making the Son of God plain and clear to mankind. Yet we are accustomed to think that training and time and brains and endless apparatus are essential to the undertaking of modern adventures, while in this, the greatest of adventures, the men were sent forth with little training, less education, and no apparatus. I want you to think about this for two reasons. Firstly, because it was an adventure. And secondly, because it was an adventure which has never ended, and is still open to all and sundry, and therefore has a very personal application for us.

It was an adventure, because its one end and object was to manifest or make clear the Son of God to mankind. I cannot think of anything which is, at first sight, more strange and unexpected, in the working of God, than His plan of using human instruments to do the work. If one had to imagine an Omnipotent Being with infinite resources, faced with the task of manifesting Himself to the world, there would seem to be such hundreds of easy ways of doing it without relying on imperfect and erratic human instruments. Yet God has, throughout His revelation of Himself, consistently used one method, that of the human agent. He has willed to reveal Himself to the world through human writers of a human book, through a class of men, or a body of people.

We can see very dimly the reason of it all, when we think about the Incarnation, for clearly it is that great fact of Bethlehem which governs the matter. God revealed Himself in human form because He would have no basis for His relationship with mankind other than sympathy. He would have no basis other than sympathy, because that alone made it possible to use human love to the full. So in all His revelation He used human instruments, in order that it might always be a sympathetic revelation ; one which had everything in common with those to whom it was made.

This line of thought may help us to understand the reason of God's method, but the only way to see the method clearly is to study the history of Christianity. In that history, year after year and century after century, the same process is seen at work, the making plain of God to men through men. The men who were being used for this purpose knew that God was using them, but they never comprehended for an instant to what extent, or perhaps their hearts would have failed them. Take, as an example, the writing of a Gospel, and read the account of it which Clement of Alexandria heard from the lips of the oldest presbyters of the Church. " The Gospel of Mark," he says, " was written in the following manner : ' When Peter had proclaimed the word publicly at Rome and declared the Gospel under the influence of the Spirit ; as there was a great number present, they requested Mark, who had followed him from afar, and remembered well what he had said, to reduce these things to writing, and after he had composed the Gospel he gave it to those who requested it of him.' " Such were the circumstances in which the Gospel, which nowadays is recognized as the very basis of the New Testament, the most important of all documents for the manifesting of the Son of God to the world, came to be written. How little the instrument knew of the greatness of his work.

Cross the bridge of time to the dark period of the middle ages, and take an episode from the life of the greatest preacher of that period, and note how God converts a town by a human instrument, to the great surprise of the said instrument. S. Bernardine of Siena, the preacher in question, thus describes the event. " One day while preaching to the best of my ability, I left the main work to God, for suddenly, and as it appeared to me accidentally, it occurred to me to dwell on that great cry for vengeance sent up by persecuted souls before the throne of God. Which words, to my great surprise, so awoke the people's conscience that they convened a meeting, whereat presided marvellous unanimity, and at which it was decided that all who had been banished from the town might return. In a few days the town gates were crowded with returning exiles, of whom their old enemies had no sooner caught sight than they ran forward to embrace them and to restore to them their goods and chattels."

These are but passing illustrations of a principle which never fails, and it is a principle which it seems most necessary to enunciate from time to time, for it lies at the root of the existence of the Church. It is not uncommon to hear it denied by thoughtless people, who generally oppose to it a truism which begs the question when they say " that nobody must come between the soul and God." That is an undeniable truth if by " coming between " you refer to an obstacle, but it is false, alike to the Incarnation and to history, if you make it refer to the human instruments, whom God uses for the work of revealing Himself to the world. He has throughout the ages used a body of human beings, the Church, and in particular a class of human agents, the priesthood, to make plain to the souls of men His message and His nature. Imperfect they have always been, full of flaws and failings, but nevertheless the means by which He taught mankind, and they are in the true line of succession to the Star of Bethlehem.

It is easy to see the imperfections of the Church to which we belong, but do not let us forget that it was the instrument which God used to save our souls and to feed us with grace. We count it a base thing for a man to speak evil of the parents who nurtured and educated his childhood, shall we count it any less base to speak evil of the Church which taught us and fed us ? Rather should we thank God for the glory of our heritage in the Church of England.

I would have you, secondly, consider the sending forth of the twelve apostles, because it is an adventure which has never ended. It is still going on ; the method of God is still at work, and through the great body of the Church, and each true member of that Church, God is still manifesting Christ to men. Don't think for one minute that it is an easy adventure. I do not suppose that the Apostles went forth with light hearts. I do not think they could have gone forth, after hearing

Christ's forecast of their fate, without the deepest fore-bodings. But still they went, conscious that their mission was more important than anything which could befall them. Wherever and whenever a man is to be God's agent, it can only be after he has counted the cost and is prepared to pay the price.

There is a curious poem, by a modern poet, called the " Sale of S. Thomas," which brings out this truth very dramatically. It describes the Apostle, S. Thomas, standing on the quayside, contemplating the ship which is to take him to India. He knows the mission upon which he is sent, but as he gazes on the ship his imagination conjures up the awful perils of the voyage. The captain of the vessel tells him of the tyrant who governs the land, and of how he has set his ambition on erecting a palace built of souls ; and of the fearful torments each craftsman has to endure who fails in the task of building it. As he listens, the cost of the venture grows greater and greater in S. Thomas' mind, till at last he feels he cannot face it, and turns away telling the captain he will not sail. At that moment a Stranger approaches the vessel, before Whose face the Apostle sinks to the ground helpless, and in awe. The Stranger claims Thomas as His runaway slave, and sells him to the captain for twenty pieces of silver, to be sold in India ; guaranteeing that he is the man who can build a palace of souls. S. Thomas, as the instrument of God, must learn to pay the price.

It needs great courage, or a strong call, to make a man God's agent to others. Is not this your own experience ? If you have ever tried to talk to others of God and of Christ and of their souls, has it not meant a fearful effort ? At the back of your own mind lay the thought of what you were, a thought which made your words seem one gigantic hypocrisy. Then there was the doubt as to what the other person would think of you, and the wound your self-respect might receive. Yet I would dare to claim that you have never made the venture, or offered yourself to God as an instrument, without either proving on the spot the need and value of your mission, or of finding it out at a later date. We then, as Christians, are the chosen means whereby God would reveal Himself to others, and if we are to be used, we have to pay a price.

But there is another side to the matter, for it is of the essence of God's method that we are *used*. I have seen a certain number of the celebrated statues of the world, but to me there is one which stands out above them all as a great reality. It is a statue erected to the memory of Phillips Brooks, Bishop of Massachusetts, and it stands in the central square of Boston. It represents the famous preacher delivering a sermon. With supreme art the sculptor has managed to suggest by the attitude and the waving folds of the gown, that a sudden inspiration has just flashed upon the man, and that in another instant he will lean forward over the pulpit with a new power in his voice, which will compel the attention of his congregation, and carry conviction to their hearts. And there behind the preacher in the shadow of the canopy, stands a majestic figure of Christ, Whose outstretched finger has rested for one moment on the shoulder of the bishop. It is a fine statue because it pictures an eternal truth. For wherever God uses human agents, He gives them His power, pours into them His Life and illuminates them with His Light. If men only realized what it meant to be used as God's instrument, what supreme joy came from the least touch of His hand, there would be no lack of volunteers for His service.

The Church has been the wonder of the world, and the chief cause of that wonder has been that with all the feebleness of its constituents, it still is filled to over-flowing with life. So long as it is God's means of manifesting Christ, it must be full of life, for every agent which God uses is provided with His Life. Nor is it any different, save in degree, with you and me. If we are prepared to pay the cost and volunteer as God's instruments, we, in spite of all our frailty and failings, shall assuredly be filled to overflowing with the power required. Never yet was there a labourer in God's vineyard who was not overpaid.

This, then, is the agelong Epiphany of Christ, wherein human stars, following their appointed courses, lead ever fresh caravans of souls to the humble and lowly Shrine of Christ, that they may learn to worship Him.

And if any doubt what part they may have in the manifestation of Christ to the world, or of their fitness or capacity, I would but have them note the last two words of this verse : " These twelve Jesus sent forth." You are the instruments of God by the *personal* call and loving command of Jesus Christ your Saviour. You can do this work if you will, because *He* and no other has sent you forth ; and if you will obey His call, you will return one day, like the Apostles, rejoicing to His feet.